MW01228213

P4P

Why Hourly Is A Failing Formula

By Mike Andes

Copyright © 2021 Michael Andes

All rights reserved.

Table of Contents

Glossary

Glossary

P4P -	Pay for Performance; an integral pay system with fixed variables in factored labor, where high performing employees see pay benefit matching higher production.
Labor Revenue -	The hourly rate charged to the customer for labor. This may be used interchangeably with Rate to Customer. Find on page 42.
Base Pay -	The guaranteed hourly wage of an employee for clocked hours. (Essentially the hourly wage) Find on page 42.
Budgeted Hours -	An accurate estimated amount of time assumed for a service or job to be completed. Find on page 44.
PNW -	Pacific Northwest; area encompassing Oregon and Washington State. This is the region where the original Augusta location was started, and where I grew up.
USP -	Unique Selling Proposition; is the one feature or the perceived benefit of a good which makes it unique from the rest of the competing brands in the market. Find on page 41.

P&L Statement -	Profit and Loss Statement; a financial statement that summarizes the revenues, costs, and expenses incurred during a specified period, usually a quarter or fiscal year. Find on page 56.
KPI -	Key Performance Indicators; are the imperative (key) indicators of progress toward a desired result. KPIs create an analytical basis for decision making, provide a focus for strategic and operational improvement and help focus attention on what matters most. Find on page 53.
Customer Acquisition Cost -	The amount of money a business spends to get a new customer. It helps measure the return on investment of efforts to grow their customer base. Find on page 80.
S Corporation -	A business that files taxes as a "Small Business" or "Self-Employed" to avoid double taxation on overhead profits when filing, and on the Profit and Loss Statement. Find on page 56.

Chapter 1

First Dollar to the Last Dime

Busy bees zipped through the blueberry bushes as I plucked dozens upon dozens of bushels. My hands were still tacky from the honey harvest the other day, the next hive was due soon too. At the time, I was 8 years old, working for 8 dollars an hour at the blueberry and honey bee farm a little less than half a mile from my house. I was able to ride my bike to work after school and on the weekends. It was a sweet gig, enough to put an eight year old on top of the world. I let my mind keep busy as the repetitive motions of my day to day there lulled and the heat sweltered on my neck. I had thought to myself;

If I could keep this up, working a dollar for every year I was old an hour- I'll be SET.

All throughout my childhood I was always looking to make a buck. I sold sandwiches and snacks to golfers that teed off near our house, I would wax snowboards during the winter. In primary school I would buy and sell candy to my peers on what I called the "Green Market" (note: a great time to buy candy is the day after Halloween when supply is high and demand ultra low). Despite my entrepreneurial adventures I also would build and remodel pallets for a local company to make extra money. Pallet building was mind numbing work and time dragged on. However, I had found myself annoyed with how differently people worked when there was a manager present versus not. When the owner or manager was around they would feverishly stack pallets, tear down and recycle old pallets, and quickly line up the studs for new pallets. When the managers left, so did the employees' work ethic. They would take long breaks, aimlessly drive around forklifts and shoot nail guns into the forest. I remember thinking, "how can this business even make a profit when half of the hours that employees work is wasted?"

When I turned 11, my brother Tim and I had the opportunity to do a landscaping project for a family friend. We had worked tirelessly for a week, and instead of offering us money, they proposed giving us $1,000.00 toward getting a little lawn care business started. Jumping at the opportunity, Andes Lawn Care was born. Little did I know that this would change the course of our careers. We used the money to buy a 21 inch residential Honda push mower, Stihl weed wacker, and a Home Depot handheld blower. We would push the equipment around our neighborhood on foot, and in the first summer made $3,000.00 in total revenue. We were rich!

The years went on and Tim (the older of the two of us) got his driver's license. We used a free green 1995 Dodge Caravan to expand our service area out of our immediate neighborhood. The driver's side of the van was smashed in, there was no AC to speak of and the back lift of the van was broken. We used a wooden stick to prop the lift door open. There were countless times that stick got knocked out while taking tools from the back, which led to it crashing down on my back. The rear seats of the van were ditched to make room for another 21 inch mower and supplies. It helped make room to haul out any debris as well. Looking back, the moss and mushrooms growing in the van's carpet was probably not up to OSHA standards.

At thirteen, I enrolled at the local college for classes. I had been saving from all of my jobs to put toward it. I performed pretty well in school, although I had to work hard for every "A" I received. Until the age of 11, I had envisioned my future career as becoming a financial advisor. I'd read books about bonds and documentaries about the stock market. A teacher of mine had pulled me aside and planted the seed of something more; that I had the potential to make a bigger impact on lives. I had become more and more interested in health and exercise, and started gravitating to the medical field. I found myself excited to become a doctor, my ideal specialty being either heart or brain surgery. The heart and brain are incredibly important in the human body, and I was drawn to their complexity as well as the challenge it brought to the table. I wanted to help change people's lives.

I wanted to make a difference.

During this time in school, I took on some part time work at the local *Anytime Fitness*. Staying true to my monetary goal, I was making $15.00 dollars an hour as a fifteen year old. I was being booked for personal training, and when working the front desk, I had the opportunity to make a commission on people signing up for memberships. From a business standpoint, the incentives were setup in a counter-productive way, giving perverse incentive to the employee. For example, at Anytime Fitness we were compensated with a $50 bonus whenever we sold a 12-month membership paid in full upfront. However, we only received $7 commission when we sold a monthly recurring 24-month membership. The key was that the average member stayed at the club for 2-3 years, resulting in the client with the LOWER lifetime value (12 month paid in full contract) gave a commission that was 7 times more than the client that signed a monthly agreement, and would lead to 2-3 times more profit for the business in the long run.

Besides this flaw in membership bonuses, it was impossible to ignore the patterns in work culture. I had begun to notice again my coworkers habits, the impulse to stand, chat and run the clock. In a sense, I get. We were there on an hourly wage. The longer something took to do, the more we were paid. Why would anyone try to cut out waste and thereby get paid less? Once I turned 18, I earned my undergraduate degree in Pre Medical Science, Health and Technology from Western Washington University.

I took a once in a lifetime opportunity to volunteer my
medical knowledge in Africa for two months. It was at
times terrifying, but also the most fulfilling experience
I've ever had. I performed life saving surgeries on gunshot
victims, delivered babies, and cared for children in the burn
unit. These individuals rarely had the money to pay for
their medical services. Many of them were orphans in the
pediatric unit I spent most of my time in. Some had been
abused, forgotten, and abandoned. However, the little care
I could give them gave them so much joy and excitement. I
remember buying several of the kids a soccer ball and a few
bottles of bubbles. They spent days happily playing with the
gift I had given them despite the fact that life circumstances
were stacked against them. The medical procedures I
performed, drugs I administered, and help I contributed
paled to the profound impact these experiences had on me.

I returned home with a new presence within myself.
I desired to continue making an impact on the lives of
those around me, I believed that would be through medical
services and surgery. With the regulations required by
medical professionals, I was again facing at least 10 years
of school to come close to doing anything I had done while
in Africa. I knew the specialty I was aiming for, and feeling
a bit discouraged, I decided to shadow some doctors and
specialties. Surprisingly, more than half the time in the
workday of a doctor is paperwork. Sitting in a solitary office
under blasting fluorescents, in front of a computer typing
and clicking, I thought back to my patients in Africa; it
was me, them, providing care and exchanging gratitude. I
realized this isn't what I'm meant for. I couldn't spend the
rest of my life pushing papers or bowing to the whims of the
pharmaceutical industry. I found it demoralizing that the
level of care and services offered was usually determined by
an insurance company, and the hands of the physician were
tied. It would be one thing if I would be able to holistically
care for a patient and draw on multiple specialties to give
them personalized medical help. However, I knew that once
I was 10 years deep into a specialty it would be unlikely
that I would have the opportunity to explore naturopathy.
It wasn't like I could switch specialties from heart surgery
to spinal surgery, and then spend a few years working on

the brain, ears, or eyes. I would be stuck in one narrow specialty, performing very specific procedures for many years. The entrepreneur inside of me dreaded this reality.

       The feedback I had gotten from peers and professors was rough when they heard I was giving up on my dreams of becoming a medical doctor. They said it was lost potential, and a big mistake. It was making me doubt my decision, but I knew it was the right move long-term. I knew my family wouldn't be mad, but I feared disappointment from other students and faculty that had supported my educational endeavors. I was reminded of when my dad had taken me to a local coffee shop back when I was enrolling in college at 13. He had told me over a steaming cup of coffee, "You know, your mom and I are proud of you? We aren't pushing you to do college this early. If you want to do this it has to be what you want and your decision. We will always be here for you, and back whatever decision you make." And even now, as we sit together at the kitchen table, and I tell them what I want to do instead, they smile. And I know I've made the right choice, and have the right people by my side.

What was my next step?

       I took up a part time position at *Anytime Fitness* as a personal trainer again, and decided to build the landscape business. My brother bought me out of Andes Lawn Care and I started my own company called **Augusta Lawn Care Services**, named after the golf course where the Masters PGA tournament is played. I was going to hit the ground running in the Pacific Northwest, in Blaine, WA. The first year in business I pulled in about $30,000 in revenue. I went full time in the spring of my second season in business. Half-way through the second year I hired a friend of mine, Joey, to work part time with me and we scaled to $200,000 in annual revenue.

      We worked 6 days a week, 10-12 hours per day. We were oblivious to the definition of holidays, vacation and overtime. In that first year we worked every single weekend without fail, and Joey was the hardest working guy I had ever met.

We grew to have around seven to eight employees, and as the owner I was being pulled more into the office side of things and out of the field. With such fast growth we were experiencing, we were pinched for profit. Most profit was going towards hiring more crew members, training and new equipment. Augusta had definitely changed from where it first started, and I could tell it wasn't the same draw that it had been for my long time friend in the business with me. Instead of being in the thick of it together, I was often removed from the physical labor and focused on doing estimates. Joey had started to mention his leaving the company, and this was something I wanted to avoid at all costs. I started offering him things like 10 percent equity of the company, and $25.00 an hour (currently he was at $17.00). I didn't realize at the time, but looking back I know these would have been huge mistakes. I couldn't afford either offer, but in my mind losing Joey would be the end of Augusta, and I needed to do everything in my power to keep him there. I think in some way, by offering these things to Joey it damaged our relationship. I can see from his perspective that *"If I'm worth that much, why weren't you already paying me this much?"* This was a huge lesson to me as a business owner, and it weighed heavily on my shoulders;

But he is worth that much.

He could have out performed two of me; an absolute asset to any business, let alone a startup that worked around the clock like madmen. This brought me back to another fundamental issue I asked myself as an employer. I needed to find a way to pay my hardest working employees in relation to how hard they work, and how much revenue they produced for the business.

The company grew feverishly, and in 2017 Augusta Lawn Care was voted as the #1 Place to Work in Whatcom County, WA. However, I found myself exhausted. The hardest part was honestly watching my team work long hours in the blazing heat during the summer and wet, cold weather during the winter. Not to mention here in

Washington, we have a solid couple months of rain. The work was grueling and besides a paycheck they had little to show for it. Worst of all, I felt the need to micromanage my team, constantly keeping an eye on them to ensure they worked hard and worked well. I had a hard time finding quality employees. I would ensure that I personally came back onsite to complete projects, do a walkthrough with the client, and collect the final payment. I tracked all my trucks with GPS to ensure that the crew stayed on task and didn't slack off, take too long between each mowing job, or stop at half a dozen gas stations throughout their daily route. I couldn't trust anyone else to send invoices, create estimates, order materials for projects, change the oil on the equipment, or complete a work change order without my involvement. I dealt with every single customer complaint, returning to the job to do unfinished work and address any issues. I would show up at the beginning of every project, and show the crew exactly what should be done according to the estimate notes. Yet, I would return days later to fix their mistakes in order to keep from losing money on a job that went way over the budgeted hours we quoted for. Again I found myself thinking, "there's got to be a better way. I need my employees to hold the same value to time and quality as I do.

I need to get my employees to think like an owner."

I made the decision to sign up the entire crew to go to a leadership conference during one winter season, to inspire them to take on the owner's mindset. We had some cash from the year saved up and I hoped that they could learn about the business side of things, to build up the team's morale after a grueling year. I wanted to show that I cared about them and their careers, beyond just the immediate profit they could bring the business. The event was two days of intense business talk about systems, team culture, and pricing landscape jobs. To have my team of approximately 10 employees there it cost me over $6,000. I paid for their admission, food, and hourly wages throughout the event.

Waking up bright and early, we set off for the

conference, the big event that I thought would unite us as a team and build a company of leaders. Rolling into the event center, we grabbed our seats in the front row of the stage. As the speakers came and went, so did my crew's interest. Many of them dozing off between the numbers and marketing strategies; only to wake up when lunch was served. I started doubting if this was really going to make an impact. I was reassured heading back to our shop however, as we all chatted about new ways we could bake our new leadership knowledge into our daily proceedings.

The conference ended and we resumed regular operations. Within a few weeks a few team members moved on to bigger and better things, and the impact I had hoped for wore off. I took a moment to understand how this must have been from their perspective. I reflected on the experience I had with past coworkers at *Anytime Fitness, the blueberry farm,* and the pallet company. We hadn't cared about efficiency, what was right for the business, or how profits could be maximized. We were just there to punch the clock, rack up time, and get a paycheck without getting fired. We didn't put thought towards how the job we were doing today would change our career prospects, or financial outcome in the future. Why did it seem like I was always pushing my employees whilst they dug their heels in, and yielded the minimum output possible?

There had to be a better way.

Pouring over the numbers in my small, dimly lit office, I knew I had to make the change. I ran calculation after calculation, a solution to all the questions I've been asking myself. How could I make sure my hardest working employees have the opportunity to shine and earn big for their efforts? How could I prevent losing employees like Joey in the future? How could I give them the power to raise their own wage without putting the business in the red? How could I make sure that when I turned my back that my employees continued to work hard with the best interest of the company in mind? How could I continue to grow the business without constantly adding to the level of stress caused from micromanagement, and babysitting of low performing employees?

The answer to all these questions were answered in the system I outline in this book: P4P.

P4P - *Pay for Performance, an all-encompassing pay system where high performing employees see compensation matching higher production and quality output.*

This will put the ball in my employees' court to do better, work harder and be more efficient. It will give the employee's the chance to learn more about business, and make more money for themselves and the business.

Fast forward a few years, this system has been tried and true at my Bellingham, WA location. The success with Augusta Lawn Care has been franchised, and now most of our locations have implemented P4P, all seeing phenomenal results. In this book, I will give you all the tools to learn, implement and grow with Pay for Performance. Although I use lawn care and landscaping to illustrate my points, P4P is here to solve the greater issue put forth by the hourly wage. It will work for nearly every industry that employs the labor of individuals, including but not limited to: contractors, cleaning and janitorial, fencing, plumbers, electricians, roofers, mechanics, delivery services, HVAC, home services; we even use it for our office staff. It's not a band-aid, it's the cure.

Chapter 2

The Faults of $/Hr

The idea of "time is money" has been so deeply engraved in our collective consciousness, that no one questions what that transaction entails, or even its validity. Looking at the history of dollars per hour, we can examine its pitfalls and strengths to build a better system.

Gaining traction in the late 1800's during the American Industrial Revolution, the mass production of goods accelerated the demand for labor in the U.S. The structure of wealthy business owners running companies from the top down set the groundwork for what we see today. The unskilled laborer was a commodity like anything else, simply a cog in the machine. As we industrialized products such as tires, furniture, and clothing little did we know that the mindset around physical labor as a means to profit was also being revolutionized.

Assembly line work is the shining example of this mentality, one worker doing a series of simple repetitive tasks to create a product they are completely disconnected from. Although dark and dingy factories with loud machines and billowing smoke stacks have been substituted with artificially-lit cubicles equipped with computer screens and potted coffee, not much has changed.

In 1938, the Fair Labor Standards Act was signed, guaranteeing the 8 hour work day, and overtime pay for employees exceeding 40 hours in a week. Before this, labor unions were created to advocate for the employee to standardize the 10-12 hour work day in as early as 1810. At the time, this was necessary to advocate for employees experiencing bodily breakdown after such tremendous, consistent strain. Unions advocated to have a minimum wage, of which was also introduced with the Fair Labor Act at .25 cents/hour. This is equivalent to $4.60 in 2020. There has been continued advocacy for the labor force, bringing us to the standards of today, and there is likely much more work to do.

Although much has been debated in terms of safety and compensation for front-line employees, little has gone into the damaging beliefs and poor results that the hourly payscale has attributed. We have somehow tried to deal with the EFFECTS instead of attacking the root problem and cause: the $/hr system. We continue to argue and fuss about how many dollars should be traded for time, how many hours should be worked in a week, and the balance of power in a capitalistic society without asking if the scale is broken and in need of replacement.

Why Labor Unions Today can be Harmful

In today's standards, there are many more regulations and protocols set in place to protect the rights and safety of employees, of which includes OSHA (Occupational Safety and Health Administration), the U.S. Department of Labor, as well as other law enforced regulations that can vary by state. There are some instances where a union can still be useful, however it is my belief that usually they act as a communication barrier, and inhibit much needed conversation up and down the chain of command in an organization/business.

In the current labor market we find ourselves, employees are considered "lazy", and employers are seen as "greedy". The use of unions is the equivalent of a band aid solution trying to patch up a failing system. They build artificial leaders to fill the rolls of middle management, putting more walls up between the owner/shareholders and the front line worker. This "us" versus "them" mentality will never motivate employees to produce more than suboptimal work.

Money and time have NO connection. They are incongruent. Increasing the time variable to perform a task does not yield more results for the business and is a poor measure for how much an employee should be compensated. Efficiency and productivity should be rewarded instead... and this is the aim of P4P.

Dollars in exchange for time perpetuates the belief that owners are extracting every ounce of profit from every employee without any regard to their well-being, or future. The mentality of owners and managers "harvesting labor" is equal to that of a farmer. This farmer constantly picks off EVERY piece of fruit from his fruit trees. In the short term he becomes more profitable. However, if he would let some of the fruit stay on the plant, the birds would come and eat the fruit, spreading the seeds throughout the land. This would lead to a multiplication of his profits. This would be compounded by the fact that now some of his time could be diverted from fruit harvesting and into cultivating the soil, pulling weeds, and fertilizing the existing plants so they actually begin to have a greater yield per plant.

In the same way, harvesting labor has become a staple of modern day business. Harvesting labor fails in a new economy with a competitive labor market and low unemployment rates. Trying to take all you can from your employees and sucking every ounce of their life out for your material gain will no longer be tolerated, and yields lower levels of productivity in the long run. Cultivating the talent within an organization leads to a happier and more productive workforce. It leads to higher compensation for the employee and greater profits for the business.

The Root

This pay system's history highlights the flaws stoked

by labor unions, perpetuating the us (owner/employer) v.s them (laborer/employee) mentality. When the first union was created, they painted a picture of an almost villainous owner that is still pushed today. This mentality has festered like a cancer on our society, resulting in resources from employees and employers spent to maintain peace through enforcement of labor unions. No one has stopped to address the root of the issue, thus no beneficial change has happened for years, leading to where we are now.

On the other side of the tug of war, you find the owner as the anchor holding executive power. This view paints owners as tyrannical rulers who are only in it for profit at any cost. As owners, we may know this isn't the case, but without a system that accurately reflects our values it is hard to be perceived otherwise. P4P allows you to go on the offense and become an asset to your team and their future. Within this system, you gain the tools and knowledge to make decisions with more precision, and apply your time to generate effective changes within the company. By bringing the team together, you create an "us" out of the "you v.s. them" mentality, and they begin to see you as a team member again.

The system you implement should do exactly that. It should organize the entire team to achieve a particular goal while eliminating waste. The ultimate tug of war is how we see the typical employee and employer relationship, both sides pulling in opposite directions generating a gridlock. Pay for Performance addresses this stalemate head on. With the energy of both sides produced being locked up in the rope, "winning" is achieved by pulling others against their will and often causing injury. The objective is to turn this dynamic into a battering ram of progress, combining the two sides' ideals and ambitions to truly create something exceptional. When employees and employers begin to PUSH in the same direction instead of pulling against each other, incredible progress can be made and the walls of impossibility can be beaten down.

This starts by giving the employees incentive to

use their heads to find creative ways of solving problems, removing the stigma that these aren't valuable members of the team.

The true tragedy of the hourly wage lies in the negative effects of incentivizing time spent and not efficiency. Employees aren't inspired to improve the process because there is no guarantee that they will actually see a meaningful impact from their contribution to improved efficiency. The avoidance of error in routinized work is rewarded the same way as taking a spelling test instead of thinking creatively to come up with unconventional solutions and ideas.

There is no immediate benefit to taking an online class to improve yourself, when you are compensated the same even if your quality of work improves. You simply have to hope that in the long run a manager or executive sees your aptitude and rewards you with more money. Similarly, there is no incentive to learn the inner workings of a business, because you are so removed from its operations. This traps the employees in a stagnant state of mind, never striving for more, all while building animosity towards the employer who they feel is holding all the power over their situation. This unbalanced power struggle between both sides can topple even the largest business if it shifts too far to either side.

The root problem with the labor industry is the dollars per hour transaction. Hiring someone based on their time spent assumes that their time holds the value. However, it is how the employee applies their skills during that time that intrinsically holds the value. In their time working, they deploy their skills to PRODUCE products and services. Hourly pay incentivises workers to provide you, the employer, with as much time as possible; and then that time is sold at a predetermined rate prior to even seeing whether the employee can produce efficiently. The employee has no immediate incentive to improve their value, and for most small businesses, the employer has little ability to ensure the time purchased from the laborer is actually increasing the value of their business.

The Employee

Not only is hourly pay harmful to your business, it's harmful to employees. Psychologists and scientists have been studying the effects that dollar per hour has on our psyche for years. What they have found is when you monetize your time, you subsequently lose the ability to enjoy leisurely time. Simply knowing how much each action you take in your day costs you by not working applies a base level of stress to your day to day life.

That trip to pick up the kids from school "costs" you $20 of time since it took one hour and that is the rate ascribed to you by your employer. Similarly, that date night with your spouse cost you $80 of time since it was the entire evening. You can't afford to read that fictional book. It will take 12 hours and therefore cost you $240 of time.

Pay for Performance allows employees to determine what matters to them and if that is finishing their work quickly to spend more time at home they should have the freedom to do so. They should also have the freedom to dictate how hard they work and get compensated fairly for their effort. The control that rests back in the hands of the employee empowers them to invest in their future providing a catalyst that accelerates them to achieve more in their life.

Automation and robotics are soon to replace labor as we know it today. Elon Musk, founder of SpaceX and Tesla was unveiling a new AI-driven, human-like robot and said, "What is the economy? At its foundation it is labor. What happens when there is no shortage of labor?"

Looking around, we can already see this in our daily lives from our Rombas (small automated vacuums) to fully automated mowers. So we have to ask ourselves, "What will I do to compete in a labor market, where price is no longer solely dictated on the amount of physical work required?" A robot won't mind working more hours. It will easily perform the mind-numbing tasks that millions of individuals do each day and rely on to put food on their tables. So why would we not train humans (while we are, at least currently, more intelligent than robots) to focus on efficiency and creative solutions instead of routine work? That way, even if the robots did commoditize labor and remove the need for routinized work, we as humans could continue to do meaningful, value-adding tasks. This is true job security. Not a law. Not a union. Not government programs or universal basic income. The ability to think outside the box, innovate, and work efficiently will never be commoditized and should be the focus of the modern workplace.

I propose that the first step to all of this is commission pay, by only providing compensation to the worker when direct profit is produced. However, the reality of the situation is most employees won't accept the terms of commission-only. Employees are looking for a stable source of income to live a sustainable life, otherwise they would probably stake out on their own path into entrepreneurship: the ultimate commission-only career. The uncertainty and risk with commission-based pay forces most entry level employees to gravitate back to hourly. So why do employers pay hourly when historically both parties have suffered from this system?

Simply put, $/hr is LAZY.
That's right. That is not a typo... I said it is LAZY!

It's a simple, trackable metric that can be budgeted for and predetermined. Labor is the largest variable expense in a business. Before a job is completed- there is no way of knowing with absolute certainty how long a job will take, because of employees pace of work, and other outside factors that cannot always be accounted for. For example in the landscaping industry, rain, a flat tire, a broken down truck, or employees taking multiple breaks at every gas station could cause a massive number of labor hours to be spent in excess of what was estimated and quoted to the customer. Dollars per hour is the lazy way of managing these variable factors. It is safe, easy, and understood by many job applicants. $/hr doesn't take much time to calculate each pay period. There are no commissions, bonuses, deductions, or percentages that must be accounted for. However, this lazy pay system encourages more waste and does more harm than the time it "saves" the employer when running payroll each week.

Beyond creating waste, the larger impact of dollars per hour is the cultural implications for your business. The system incentivises workers to take an exorbitant amount of time while completing tasks, because they are compensated equally no matter how efficient they actually are. It fuels the need for middle level management to watch over employees and force them to stay productive, thereby stripping the employees of the freedom or drive to improve. I believe that no employee (let alone your top performers) want to have a manager constantly watching over their shoulder, and monitoring their every action in the name of "loss prevention" and "quality control."

Dollars per hour perpetuates falsehoods in the value of an employee. Unfortunately, front line employees are typically seen as "just hands" or a cog in the machine; a commodity that can be replaced. I am always amazed how in a growing company "management" begins to think that strategizing and planning an employee's output makes the business successful, but this makes them lose touch of what the Customer is ACTUALLY paying for. The reality of the situation is that front-line employees ARE the business. In most cases they are the only ones generating revenue, while the overarching goal of the business is to organize their labor as efficiently as possible.

In the current dynamic between employer and employee, we find at each end of the rope an anchor that locks them in place. For the team, this anchored person is the one who knows that the owner can't afford to lose them. They get all the complaints from the front line team and are the ones who push on their behalf for change. In an hourly position this team member is the enemy of the owner, but this is the last thing you want as they are the ones with the power and knowledge to actually incite meaningful change. Fostering a relationship with the employee everyone tells their complaints to gives you a glimpse of what work is actually like on the front lines. Their anchor can be your biggest asset but unless they can trust you and feel they are working in a fair system, they would never consider voicing the complaints of the team in a constructive light.

I believe that people innately have a drive to problem solve and use their head as much as their hands. This "head" work has been revered by some as the "harder" work that managers do. Employees are expected to do as they are told with little input or discussion about how the work could be done more efficiently, but why should they care anyway if they aren't being incentivized to come up with time-saving ideas? Little do owners realize that the best ideas and solutions come from those CLOSEST to the problem, and that is usually the front line laborers. Unless high performing employees are given the opportunity to be compensated for their "harder" work, working harder will lose its appeal. By changing the rules of the pay system game, we inevitably align the goals of the business and employee around cutting waste and increasing profit.

The Chainsaw Massacre

Before P4P, I ran your average lawn care business. There truly wasn't much that set us apart from anyone else. Although the business did over $1,000,000 in annual revenue I was still the bottleneck to every sale, every Customer complaint, and every project. I worked long days, evenings, and weekends. The goal of P4P is to free the owner from the shackles of daily operations, and allow the front line team to take on more accountability and autonomy without micromanagement. The main problem I had stemmed from the demand of project management. Routine work such as mowing and weeding jobs could be done without my involvement and placed on a recurring schedule. However, large hardscaping and project jobs not only required a longer sales cycle, but on the day of the job starting I would visit the property and walk through the site and job notes with the crew.

This created a logistical problem as the business grew, since we were constrained by how many projects could be done in one day. We would have staggered start times of 7 AM, 7:30 AM, 8 AM, and 8:30 AM just so that I could show all the projects to their respective crews and orient them to the job. After my morning job briefings and walkthroughs I would spend most of my day going to meet prospects and selling more jobs. At the end of the day I would spend a few more hours (typically 4PM-6PM) going back to job sites and walking through completed projects with the client to ensure their satisfaction. I was the grand master of the circus making sure everyone played their part, knew their role, and executed flawlessly. I assumed this was what a 7-figure business owner's life entailed... constantly chasing the next big job while feverishly trying to install the work as promised at a high standard of quality, and at a decent profit margin.

I decided that in order to grow the business further something would have to change. I would take a video during the estimate, detailing every part and step of the job, as it was still fresh in my mind after talking to the prospect. I would save the video on file, and then once the customer accepted their proposal, I would ensure the crew had the video as well as the job notes to make certain the job was done to specification. We called these "Project Management Videos", and it freed up my mornings from countless job briefings with the crew. I wish I could say this revelation came to me as some sort of eureka moment but it was a hard lesson I had to learn because of a failure... from a time back when we didn't have project management videos. We now infamously call this event the "The Chainsaw Massacre".

My main field leader at the time was part of the Army Reserve; His name was Mason, and was a very smart and reliable guy. I had taken on a job which was way out of our typical scope of work, but I knew with his expertise and can-do attitude we could get it done. It was a simple split rail fence replacement. The catch was there was about 500 yards of fencing that needed to be cut down, hauled to the dump, and replaced with stained cedar lumber. We're talking about a $30,000 job! There's no way I was going to turn that down. The job was pretty simple: rip out the old rotting posts and rails, dig holes, replace them with the new lumber, give it a stain and call it good.

As part of the Army Reserves, Mason was the OIC (officer in charge) of twelve weekend sessions of training per year. He would be the project manager upon his return from "drill." Because I knew my Monday morning schedule would be filled with other job briefings and walkthroughs, I took Mason to the split rail fence job the Thursday prior. After explaining the project, we headed our separate ways, and scheduled the job to start 4 days later when he got back from drill.

Monday morning arrived, and Mason's training had run late the night before. He essentially drove through the night to beat the crew to the job site. It was dark, he was sleep deprived, but he and the team got started cutting down the old fence.

What could go wrong?

Well apparently a lot! I had finished taking care of things on my list that morning, and went to swing by the split rail fence job to see how far they got in the first couple hours. The plan was to use chainsaws to cut out the old rails that lay horizontally between posts. I started to get a pit in my stomach as I drove past section after section still intact. By this point, they should have at least cut the railing up. Where was the pile of old rails? Where was the crew?

Then I see it. Half way down the road was a trail of cut railing and sprinkling of old posts. However, this was not the fence we were hired to replace, this was the neighboring HOA's fence! They looked exactly the same along the long, straight road and as I pulled up to see the team working away oblivious to the situation, I also saw HIM. A storming home owner, red in the face, shaking with rage and about to start a rampage. I jumped out of my truck, flying past the startled crew. This guy was beyond mad, he was furious! A barrage of threats and cursing accompanied with enough spit I felt like I needed a shower. After he expelled all of his energy trying to bury me and my team six feet under, I told him we would replace the railings and get this whole mess sorted away. Although still enraged, he accepted and I thought we dodged a bullet. We wouldn't be making money but at least we wouldn't have some rich guy bringing down the hammer on my small business.

So I talked to the crew and filled them in on the situation. I couldn't be mad at them, but man it was hard for us all to digest the mistake we just made; especially for our project manager, Mason, whose pride was shaken for sure. The plan was simple, we would take the old rails from the fence we were SUPPOSED to remove and use those on the neighboring fence we accidentally cut down. Fortunately, we had not removed the posts from the neighboring fence so I figured this could all be resolved in 2 days worth of work. We had to do this quickly because we had our actual client who was oblivious to our mistake and just thought we were late on our project.

So I enlisted the help of my mom to cook up some prime rib, so we could bolster some spirits and work a solid twelve the next day and catch up. Though the crew was still pretty wounded by the misunderstanding, we still had high hopes that we could get the job done profitably. Working alongside the team to get this done, drill on one hand, and tasty ribs in the other, we worked into the night to get all the rails in. As I was thinking to myself that the crisis was barely avoided, I saw a good ol' homeowner rushing back out, fists in the air cussing so loud that the neighborhood cats started ducking for cover.

Again we clashed, of course he was under the impression that us, the little landscaping company, was out here doing charity work for him and his multi-millionaire neighbors. He expected us to replace the rails with brand new cedar lumber. Furthermore, he expected not only the rails but the entire fence including the posts, gravel foundations, and gates be replaced! What killed us was that he waited till we screwed in the entire 500 yards of recycled railing to bring up that we had "robbed him" and that we were "con artists". With my pride on the line and the team there with me I had no choice but to bend to his whim, especially if I expected to have any chance of working in this area again. So I had to call our real client and tell them their job was off, we would be installing their neighbors fence with the materials we had promised to them, and their job would be delayed until we could get more cedar- which could be weeks.

This was cataclysmic, this job went from $30,000.00 to NEGATIVE $30,000.00 overnight. This was the nail in the coffin of our profits for that calendar year, since we didn't have much cash in the bank after a long year of growth. We got the job done but no one was happy, the crew felt defeated and Mason was in ruins. He came to me asking to pay it off in his paychecks, but in my eyes it wasn't his fault. It was my fault that this sort of error could take place. It was my fault that I couldn't be there Monday morning to show him the job. He had told me later his dad had written him a note of affirmation the night of the Chainsaw Massacre, and he kept it in his wallet to read daily for almost a year.

We started project management videos right after this, and it sparked the fire of change in Augusta. We had to let the pain of this experience change the way we thought about management, organization, and employee responsibility. No matter where you are along the ladder of success in this industry there is always something to be learned, places to improve, and terrible customers to deal with. Sure, with better communication this could have all been avoided, but nothing can change the past. We employ HUMANS in the labor industry, not brainless "cogs". We invite this opportunity to see the humanity in the people within our team, and choose to grow despite any negative impacts. Though not many of the original crew remain from when this event happened, the memory and implications have impacted every single person to follow. We made it out alive, and The Chainsaw Massacre will live on infamously forever at Augusta.

It was a reminder that for most small businesses the OWNER is the bottleneck. The business will only grow to the extent that the owner is willing to expand and grow their skill and knowledge depth. There are 5-figure entrepreneurs that will never grow a business past $100,000 in annual revenue. There are 6 and 7-figure entrepreneurs. There are also entrepreneurs that are able to build multi-billion dollar companies. At the end of the day, we as owners MUST realize that the constraint is US. The constraint is our ability to make difficult changes. The constraint is our willingness to learn, gain knowledge, and do the deep work on ourselves to grow as leaders. The Chainsaw Massacre only revealed how dependent the business was on my personality, organizational skills, and experience. This is great for an owner's ego since without you everything falls apart. However, this is the wrong behavior or mentality for the sustainability of your business, your employees, or your Customers. Only you can push your limiting beliefs and boundaries from a 7 figure entrepreneur to an 8 figure entrepreneur. To do that will take change. In order for Augusta to grow past $1,000,000 in revenue I realized that I must create systems (such as project management videos) to allow my Team to take ownership of their individual jobs without my involvement. I paid the price of this lesson, but heard the principle loud and clear when my insurance dropped us and our premiums tripled because of the cost to replace the split rail fence. P4P will absolutely be hard to implement. It will be extremely difficult. It will push you to think in new ways, but is required to grow your business to the place you have always dreamed. Change is hard, but change is necessary.

Chapter 3

What is P4P?

Regardless if your business is thriving or struggling financially, P4P is the change your company needs. For small companies looking to expand, it allows them the fortitude of reliable profit margins to accelerate growth safely. Larger companies with more employees will benefit 20-30% from labor efficiencies gained, while removing the owner from being the bottleneck of daily operations, all while putting more money in the pockets of the employees. The time given back to the owner due to the increased level of employee accountability, allows for future growth as they focus on sales and hiring instead of delivering materials to job sites, juggling client meetings, or micromanaging the crew. With the mindset of a P4P system, owners can work on the business while the system manages the behavior of the crew that they once maniacally watched over.

P4P acts as the defense allowing you to go on the offense.

This dynamic is strengthened when pillars of trust, honesty, transparency and communication are built upon a foundation of cooperation. Without these pillars, Pay for Performance will fail and your employees will leave. If your work isn't steady enough or budgeted well, they won't see the benefits of P4P. Similarly, if they can't trust your calculations of the compensation each day, then your team will think you're cheating them. This isn't a band aid solution, it is a cultural shift in your business that when implemented correctly, will create a ripple effect of progress and improvement.

If it was as simple as flipping a switch, most businesses would transition. Unfortunately, this leads to exactly why most people stick to hourly wages. It's easy; hours worked times pay rate equals wages earned. P4P strives to keep this level of simplicity, but it is inherently more complicated. This was the root of my hesitation when originally building P4P, I couldn't have the cost of calculating compensation be more than the time saved in labor. Beyond the backend complications, the concept of Pay for Performance is so contradictory to our current hourly pay structure, that I was worried about getting pushback from my team; considering the fact that most laborers don't like the idea of commission-based pay or salary. In most States physical laborers on the front lines are not even eligible to receive salaries, as $/hr is required for their safety. Breaking the cultural and mental mold of hourly is the largest hurdle to successfully implement P4P. Building the groundwork for a cooperative environment where your high performers can work hard while you take the mantle of educator, will be our first steps to building this new system.

P4P sounds too good to be true, a magic way to pay your employees based on how hard they work without forfeiting your own profits or quality of work. Well, the catch is that this isn't easy. Implementing P4P will change the entire fabric of how you do business and takes a lot of hard work and dedication to implement. However, it is a system that rewards innovation, produces valuable team members, eliminates micromanaging and builds a culture of cooperation and determination. Pay for Performance is a different way to pay and a different way of running a profitable business, and brings so much more value to the table. So what is P4P?

Employees receive a percentage of the labor revenue they earn for the business.

It's as simple as that, and that is the key to its success. Simplicity is the first step to creating a functioning system. The layman's breakdown is the employee gets a percentage of the labor revenue they complete. This is calculated in parallel to their base pay. Base pay, as we call it, is the minimum dollars per hour ($/hr) of clocked time for an employee. It is the minimum wage that an employee can earn regardless of their performance. Each day base pay is calculated and each day P4P is calculated. At the end of the pay period, the employee gets the higher of the two. In a sense, the employee is protected from ever dropping below their base wage, while the employer is protected from spending more on wasted labor, or giving raises to undeserving employees. The ability to generate the performance dollars rests in the hands of the employee. The delta between base pay and P4P is what we refer to as "performance dollars" since it is the bonus earned when efficiency is high. If they are able to work faster than budgeted hours and reduce non-revenue producing actions such as drive time, they instantly reap the benefits of their hard work from the money they directly save the business. In the process, the goals and aspirations of the company and the employee are aligned and the walls between the sides slowly fall away. The employee can invest in improving their skills and honing their craft while receiving a tangible benefit for doing so each and every day. The owner is released from the struggles of micromanaging, and can be freed to allocate their time back on the business.

As business owners, we struggle with portraying the importance of making profit as a true goal for the employee. This stems from the fact that to them they put in "all this work" and never see a tangible difference. The stereotypical laborer is the clearest example of this. Typically portrayed as lazy, uneducated, and unskilled, they are no more than a product of their environment. Placed in low paying jobs without freedom or incentive to innovate, they complacently jump between jobs and lack the power to make an impact in their life. P4P directly addresses this by removing the ceiling of their potential while giving the power back to the employee. By paying them a percentage of the revenue they generate, they finally see direct, tangible correlation between their hard work and profits.

This motivation and freedom allows them to use their creativity to innovate and adapt. Without a cap on their potential, they can continually improve themselves and thus, the company will see growth as well. When efficiency becomes the focus, the ripple effect of that change is felt throughout our entire lives. Looking at time through this lens you can work a 6 hour day, with the productivity typically seen in a 8 hour day. In this scenario, your hard work is rewarded by allowing you more leisure time or more time available to earn more money. The key is giving the employee the power to make that decision and providing incentives that align your goals with theirs. If they want to increase their earning power they can take time to improve their skills through courses, certification, or watching YouTube videos to figure out more efficient ways to perform their work.

Since we implemented P4P at Augusta, I have never been approached by someone for a raise. This is typically an awkward conversation for an employer, and the employee is no more comfortable initiating it. If someone were to come to me asking for a raise I would simply tell them that they have the power to learn and become more efficient at the job, which will have an immediate impact on their paycheck. I would tell them to learn from and shadow other employees in the company that are excelling and making lots of performance dollars. I would encourage them to watch online videos to improve their skill set and performance. They have no excuse of "I am worth more" when their performance says otherwise, and their peers are making significantly more each day on their paycheck.

As a business owner, the idea of shifting power to employees sounds like a nightmare and in a $/hr system, it is. Pay for Performance breaks down those conventions by balancing quality and quantity by providing you, the business owner, with the tools necessary to efficiently lead. The initial misconception is that P4P focuses on speed sacrificing quality and leading to problems down the road. However, enforcing quality is imperative to running a business no matter the pay structure, P4P places the enforcement on the shoulders of the employees and implements systems to ensure quality standards are met.

Finding good employees continues to be one of the hardest dilemmas plaguing the home service industries. Once you do find decent workers, trying to pay them an increasingly higher livable wage cuts even deeper into revenue, but is required to retain them. However, by paying them a percent of the revenue they are generating for the company, you can ensure that your profits are consistent and not dictated by outside forces. In my chemistry classes in college I learned that all matter moves towards entropy: a state of disorder. In an organization of individuals the same is true. Left to their own devices without accountability, metrics, and goals employees will usually default to the lowest permissible standard. The P4P system is the police that enforces the rules of the game and enables high performers to thrive, whilst shedding lazy and unproductive members of the Team. Once an employee's actions are directly tied to their paycheck, they begin managing their own time more effectively and efficiently. The system is the enforcement instead of an overbearing and authoritarian boss.

You can take a deep breath knowing that if the team is on their phones or runs off to the gas station they probably have a good reason for doing so, and if not you aren't taking the financial hit from their wasted time. This washes away the perception of you as the greedy business owner, always watching over the shoulders of your crew, inspecting their work, and skeptically double-checking their whereabouts throughout the day. Trust me, they hate you doing it and any high performing employee doesn't want to be micromanaged.

P4P will also provide a safety net for employees if they are having a bad day, the weather is horrible, or they are brand new by providing a base pay per clocked hour. When you are advertising for open positions you need the base pay to be high enough to attract employees and give a sense of security; however, you want it to be low enough to where the performance dollars make a good chunk of their pay. Job applicants are numb to the promise of bonus incentives since they are usually forgotten promises after the interview process. Therefore, entry-level applicants usually compare jobs using $/hr as the primary metric. The goal as your business grows is that your company gains a reputation, and employees hear that your P4P system is NOT empty promises or a carrot and stick approach to management. However, until the time when most of your job applicants are referred by existing employees and know about your company culture, the base pay is an important recruitment tool that should be carefully determined. Base pay also allows you to lower the floor of pay slightly, ensuring that you avoid taking the hit from employees stagnating or under performing. You don't want the base pay so high that people are happy with hitting it every single paycheck. Usually this behavior will be snuffed out by other high performing crew members that depend on the team to complete jobs efficiently. Still, you can't make the base pay so appealing that no one wants to push for performance dollars.

It shows up time and time again that the older employees stallout at their higher wages that they've been provided, simply for being around for a while. This system keeps them motivated and allows them to employ their expertise to continue upward wage mobility. It is simply NOT FAIR that a hungry, motivated, hard working 19 year old does twice as much work, makes twice as much money for the business and see half as much money returned, as the 40 year old that has worked 15 years with the company, and slacks off throughout the day. It is also not fair that an employee that kicks butt all day long, gets to work early with a plan for their day, and earns $1000/day in profit for the business; is making $5 more per hour, compared to the guy that shows up one minute before start time, aimlessly works throughout the day without intention, and costs more to have on payroll than his $15/hr paycheck.

P4P finally gives you a way to pay your employees exactly what they're worth. Using the numbers to dictate their pay eliminates the guessing game and favoritism that ruins businesses. No one is happy in the situation that the boss's best friend or relative is making double the other workers and working half as hard. That said, it keeps you accountable as the business grows to know your numbers, and be prepared to back up those calculations when scrutinized.

So where is all this money coming from? In the beginning, this sounds like a congressional budget where the funding behind the initiative is shady and complicated, but this couldn't be further from reality. It's no secret that running a business comes with waste, whether that's in unbillable hours like commuting or wasted material.

Few people realize that one of the largest forms of waste is generated from unmanaged labor. To an hourly employee, it makes sense to push a job into the following day because they'll get paid to drive back and forth again the next day. If it is blazing hot, who wouldn't take that option when they can drive 30 minutes back and forth from the job in an air conditioned vehicle? That wasted money is exactly what is used by P4P to encourage employees to take a different perspective to working. Shifting this perspective allows the employee to see behind the curtain at all the money essentially going down the drain. Anyone in this position starts to brainstorm what they can do to affect those dollars, especially if they know they'll get a part of it. P4P places the owner and employee in the same position of trying to eliminate waste but more importantly both profit from that effort.

After P4P had been implemented at Augusta, employees were taking the initiative to improve efficiency. It was the first spring on the new system for our employees, when our office received a call from a customer.

She was very frazzled on the phone, was stuttering and couldn't catch her breath. She was talking about some disheveled man that was running around her house. After seeing his signature Augusta yellow shirt, she thought of her service with our company and called. She trembled, "There's a man with long hair running all over my yard! He has one of your shirts on, I think he might be trying to get into my backyard!"

We had to reassure her that this was one of our employees, and that we like to work fast. That particular employee stopped by around lunch time, and the office staff immediately knew what had frightened the customer. His long hair about shoulder length, had mud in it, was slightly tangled and frizzled from the rain. He looked like he had just emerged from a jungle!

That was the day he learned how to use a hair tie, and we luckily haven't got another call like that since. That being said, he did rank as the top employee on Pay for Performance that week! These types of "complaints" from Customers are much better than the ones that say "your crew has been sitting in my driveway for 30 minutes without doing any work." I'll take the complaints that my crew is working fast, running, and getting the job done "too fast." Thank you P4P!

Chapter 4

How to Implement P4P

Pretending that money is not important to your employees or your business is crazy. To your business, cash is the oxygen it needs to survive. The same way that a scuba diver carefully measures and plans their oxygen supply for a dive, a business owner must carefully calculate the amount of cash needed to run and grow the business. To your employees, cash is the reason they show up each day. Embrace the fact that without a paycheck none of your Team would work. So let's not try and sidestep the issue or brush it under the mat. Money is an essential part of life and there is nothing wrong with providing so much value to others that you amass a lot of money. Money simply exposes and magnifies the true values a person has. A person that loves to give and help others will simply do MORE OF THAT when they achieve riches. A person that hurts others and manipulates will simply do MORE OF THAT when they attain riches.

I wanted to give my Team a clear path to get ahead in life and make more money. Just telling them to "work hard and one day you will get a raise or promotion" seemed like an obscure and intangible path to success. It was like telling someone to find their way to the top of a forested mountain but not giving them a map, compass, or trail head marker. P4P gave the rules, the boundaries, and the demarcated path to making more money and succeeding inside the company. The first step to implementing a system like P4P is taking ownership of the role of a trailblazer. The trailblazer has to cut their way through low-hanging branches, over raging rivers, and around obstacles and gullies. They take the risk of falling or injury if they take the wrong step, however, without the trailblazer those that come behind them will never have a clear path to the top of the mountain, where the views are surreal and the journey is worth taking. If you as the owner of your business have the desire to help your employees get to the next place in their career and financial future, you must be willing to do the hard work of exploring your numbers, cutting down "trees" of waste, and fording the "rivers" of crucial conversations. You will be misunderstood, you will make mistakes, and you will get hurt as you implement P4P and blaze a trail for future employees to follow.

But the view at the top is worth the climb.

Nothing is a given in business, and without hard work nothing will get done. Implementing P4P is no different. Think of it like this: If you want to build a great house you must first start with pouring a solid foundation. To build a solid business you must use tried and true systems. I look at P4P as the rebared foundation for every great home service business. A concrete foundation made with shoddy workmanship and no rebar gives an outward appearance of stability while building, and might look just fine throughout the entire building process. However, when the house is nearly DONE and the roof is being put on you have a decision to make. Should you install asphalt shingles or heavy duty steel shingles that weigh 20X as much? The heavy duty shingles will last for a lifetime but the increased mass of the steel will collapse the foundation that was built without rebar. Therefore asphalt shingles are chosen, everything looks fine... at least for now.

Your business is the same way. Without P4P being implemented, and the entire business being constructed on top of it, the business owner is less likely to be able to leave day-to-day operations. The owner leaving daily operations is equivalent to a heavy roof being put on top of the house, and stress testing everything below it. If an owner leaves a business and the heavy weight of that decision is put on the business without P4P to govern efficiency, the house will come crumbling down. That is why most home service millionaires continue to work 50-60 hours IN their business every week. They have settled for the asphalt shingles. They have settled for the fact that without them the business would fall apart and they are correct, it will. They also do not want to do the demolition required to restart the construction of the business from the ground up. So what do they do? They settle for the asphalt shingles, they stay IN the business; until one day when a massive tornado comes and tears the roof apart, exposing the rest of the house and it's contents to the rain and elements. The same thing happens in a business. The business person working in their business 50-60 hours a week without systems begins to have all the trappings of a posh and successful entrepreneur. The business is making money, they work hard, and everything looks great just like the asphalt shingled house. Then one day a tornado comes in the form of a family death, an unexpected medical emergency, or a relationship breaking up. Because the roof was not built solid and the business was never built on systems, the personal life of the business owner is wrecked. Once they have hit rock bottom and the roof has been torn off, it negatively affects the lives and livelihoods of all their family and their employees, especially those inside the business.

So if you are sick and tired of asphalt shingles, bring out some TNT, let's blow up your business and let's restart the construction of the house on the solid foundation of P4P. Let's build a business that is safe for you, your employees, and their families to build a future inside of.

If a solid foundation to your business is P4P the concrete forms are your company's numbers. It is a requirement to know these numbers BEFORE you start pouring the concrete of P4P. We'll look at determining your labor revenue, base pay, customer rate, and budgeted hours. Beyond the numbers, you'll need the tools to successfully lead your team, ensure quality, and confidently determine your calculations.

Building the foundation to implement P4P into your business:

1. Reflection:

Reflection involves you looking at yourself as the owner, and taking a birds eye view of your company as whole. Once you have a grasp on what your current standing is, then you'll be prepared to lead your team through the transition. By taking this approach, you can be confident in your numbers and have the information to educate your team along the way. Keep in mind that there is no half baked version of Pay for Performance, so understanding the system in its entirety is key to applying it to your business.

Ready yourself for open criticism. To open the doors of communication, there will always be positive and negative feedback. It can be hard to get this kind of communication, but it is better to have the feedback of the team, than have something fester that you are unaware of.

Be prepared to give trust, to get trust returned. You must be able to trust your team to essentially manage their own time in order for them to implement and want to improve to beat budgeted hours. You must trust that they will not hurry through jobs, and result in losing Customers due to low quality work. They will have the trust that you do not manipulate the numbers and calculations of P4P on the backend.

Make sure the current processes are steadfast, and rely as little as possible on opinion based metrics. As much as possible, our goal is to rely on predetermined, number-driven data. Numbers don't lie, they are objective. We must rely on those instead of subjective feelings, expectations, or standards.

2. Customer Rate:

If you are just getting started or you tend to have an hourly rate that varies between projects, a good place to start is to work backwards. Starting with how much you need to pay each employee to attract quality candidates can then determine what rates you need to charge the customer. We talk about determining the base rate you pay employees soon.

This leans back onto your USP: Unique Selling Proposition. What makes you different from everyone else? This might be that you're just a young kid starting out and saving for college, or that you provide a higher quality service and better communication than the competition. Using your USP gives you the tools to justify your higher prices and garner a customer base that is willing to pay a premium price.

What sets Augusta apart, i.e. what is our USP? Professionalism. In lawn care, there is a stereotype of someone playing too loud of music while working, smoking on the job, lacking communication skills, they're hard to get ahold of, and often do not have a uniform look. We're filling this need in the industry. All of our employees are drug free, we are insured, and have a standard professional uniform. We have staff that will answer the phone quickly and respond to emails in a timely manner. Not to mention, our service team has some great communication skills and are efficient.

Although you do not invoice based on the number of hours spent on the job (clocked hours), you will create the estimate/quote based on the number of Budgeted Hours expected for the job to be completed. Billing your customers this way gives you the information to accurately determine your base pay and your labor revenue.

3. Labor Revenue:

You need to be at the point where you can determine your labor revenue on each job. When any of us start out, we are mostly ball-parking jobs based on loose contextual clues at best, but as our business matures we learn to break down jobs into averaged estimated costs for labor and materials. We can then run that against a premium to the customer as a form of overhead recovery and profit.

The entry level to successfully implementing Pay for Performance requires you to determine how much you are charging the customer hourly; you then can break down your labor revenue.

Labor Revenue = Budgeted Hours x Rate to the Customer

Using labor revenue as the basis in which pay is determined, ties wages as close to performance as possible. This is one goal P4P sets out to accomplish. Therefore, this is aligning the goals of the team and owner, to eliminate waste and improve inefficiencies in the business.

It's important to note the extra cost to the client here as well. Outside factors of labor that include materials, delivery fees, equipment rentals; these should be added to the cost of the client to avoid eating into the revenue.

4. Base Pay:

The next step is determining what percentage of labor revenue the business is already spending on labor. Most people don't track their labor revenue separately before starting this system. In this case, you'd want to run the numbers in the background for a few months to determine your baseline. If you know how much labor revenue was earned last year, simply divide that by the number of clocked hours on payroll and you will have an average to START with. Usually your base pay rate will be 10-20% below this number (to lower the floor slightly for under performers). Also, take all the direct cost of labor and divide that by the total labor revenue. Multiply that by 100 and you will have what percent of labor revenue you spent on wages. Typically the % that you will give to employees on P4P will be 0-5% lower than this number.

Calculations for Finding Historical Numbers:
1.) Labor Revenue Earned Last Year / Clocked Hours = Average $/hr
   Minus 10-20% = Starting Point for Base Pay
2.) Total Labor Cost / Total Labor Revenue x 100 = % of Labor Revenue Paid to Employees

Determining "base pay" can be as simple as using minimum wage for your region. However, that severely underestimates the power of running a base rate on the P4P system. Base pay offers you, as the business owner, leverage in the labor market to attract quality talent and stay competitive in an environment, where $/hr is still the thing entry level employees look at first since it is "guaranteed money."

The importance of having a good base pay hadn't been more apparent until the labor shortage of 2020. Workers had the ability to deny low paying, entry-level, or laborious work due to government stimulus, and unemployment checks rolled out to support the economy throughout the Coronavirus pandemic. This shined light on the labor trend, where laborers are moving into employment away from strenuous, tedious and sometimes dangerous jobs. Often, these employers can't afford to continuously raise rates to attract these workers. Base rate is the hourly amount that acts as the floor for what your employees can earn, and is the standard we compare our P4P numbers against. It also provides an attractive stability for the labor market employee. Again, if they wanted risk they would simply start their own venture and become an entrepreneur instead of working for you on a 100% commission basis.

Calculating what your base pay should be is fairly simple, the goal is to give the employee less than 25% of what we are charging the customer. This is a benchmark I see consistent with high profit margin service businesses. Again, only your LOWEST performing employees will hit this base pay number. High performers will be making much more than base pay.

Hourly Rate to the Customer	Base Pay Maximum Recommendation
$60/hr	$15/hr
$65/hr	$16.25/hr
$70/hr	$17.5/hr
$75/hr	$18.75/hr
$80/hr	$20/hr
$85/hr	$21.25/hr

5. Budgeted Hours:

Budgeted hours is an important financial pillar of the Pay for Performance system, and is particularly catered to the labor industry. To be able to break down exactly how much time it should take to complete a job, you can accurately bill the client, generate labor revenue numbers, and allocate the necessary resources (in this case time and labor) to provide the promised outcome on a specific schedule. Budgeting correctly takes the most experience

Fig.1

to achieve, and is the point where most investors that buy their way into the industry face hardships. This can be avoided by hiring a general manager, someone with experience in the field, a strategy that we've employed successfully multiple times to build new Augusta franchises. At the end of the day the estimator MUST be able to accurately predict the budgeted hours on a job or else all confidence in P4P will be lost with the crew.

That being said, every front line employee on P4P is maniacally watching budgeted hours. The first thing they do when they arrive at a project is judge the estimator as to whether or not the budgeted hours are sufficient. They care because it has a direct impact on THEIR paycheck. Once a crew member has been on P4P for several months and has got in the habit of watching the clock and judging their own performance it is a relatively easy transition into an estimator role. The simpler your services are and the lower the level of skill required the faster a front line employee can become an estimator, assuming they have good communication skills and a personality for sales.

Typically, the estimator position is one of the highest paid positions for the highest skilled employee with the most experience; yet, they bring no revenue into the business and are an overhead cost. This is not required once ALL team members know how to accurately predict budgeted hours and materials. To this day, our estimator position at our first Augusta location has been operated by an 18 year old, 19 year old, and no one with more than 3 years of landscape experience. The position gets some profit sharing (covered later in the book) but on average makes less than our employees in the field.

The balance when budgeting hours is to ensure there is enough time allotted to your team to finish the work efficiently, and beat the budgeted hours and earn P4P, while not raising the rates so high that the customer doesn't accept the job. In theory, you can't budget too many hours for a job, but with each hour added the total price increases. You are more likely to lower your close ratio and lose customers if you are charging too much for the job.

It's important to note that budgeted hours are strictly internal information. This needs to be enforced between you and your crew. If your team tells the customer that there are two budgeted hours on a job but then leaves after just one, the customer will inevitably call demanding lower rates, or blaming the crew for rushing the job. The point of providing the team with the budgeted hours and the labor revenue for the job is to equip them with the information to set goals and run the numbers themselves; not to be shared with the customer. This is also why I recommend never telling Customers your hourly rate on an estimate and just charging them based on how long the job takes. First, the client might flip out if they are told they are being charged $80-100/hr for manual labor jobs. Second, you don't want the client putting your crew on a stopwatch, and becoming "the boss" that is watching over their shoulder. Charging the client a predetermined dollar amount allows the client to know the final price before the job begins, and eliminates surprises. More importantly, it allows your crew to have a targeted number of hours to beat on P4P, and make performance dollars.

Once you've laid out the foundation above, we can now determine what percentage of labor revenue can be given to the employees on P4P.

A keynote to take into consideration, is that once P4P is ACTUALLY being applied to your teams paychecks, they will usually improve efficiency by 20% - 30%. So do not be discouraged if you run the numbers from your last year's wages and realize that 40-50% of labor revenue was paid to employees and you have been unprofitable.

There are two reasons why a business would implement P4P, and the reason you're doing it will determine what % of labor revenue you give to employees. The first reason you would implement P4P, is because your business is unprofitable. The second reason is less about the money for yourself, and more about the accountability you actually want your employees to make MORE money. This is important to note to ensure that you don't have resentment after implementing P4P. For example, let's say you run the numbers from the past year and 40% of labor revenue went to wages, but you couldn't make any profit. If you implement P4P where 40% of labor revenue goes to the employee, you will probably end up being resentful since most of the profits gained from the new pay structure will end up in the pockets of your employees when they become 20-30% more efficient. This however, might be just fine if you already had a healthy profit margin, wanted your employees to be more profitable, and where the financial goals and obligations are being well met for the business and personally.

Consistency is imperative when delegating a percentage of labor revenue to Pay for Performance dollars.

If you are constantly adjusting the rate in which P4P is paid out, then it is no different then paying hourly. The power dynamic would still be in your hands and the employees would feel less autonomy to make more money, because they feel the game is rigged against them. They will think, "If I make too much on P4P, the owner will just lower the percent cut I get, there's no point in trying to make more money." With that in mind, it is much better to err on the side of caution when determining the percent of labor revenue that goes to the employee. If a business is struggling, we typically suggest starting at 25 or 30%. This is an easy number for the team to calculate in their heads as they are getting a 4th of the labor revenue for that job; then down the line increasing that to 33%. We have found that 33% is the golden ratio when it comes to implementing P4P in the lawn care and landscaping industry. It comes out to a third of labor revenue, which gives your team an easy benchmark to run the numbers in their head. They simply know that they make % of any labor revenue they complete. It also provides the business enough headroom to make a profit while the team is consistently making performance dollars. Although the industry you are in may be different with more materials, equipment, etc, just remember that those do not come into play for P4P. The employee ONLY gets a cut of the LABOR REVENUE so as long as your base pay is ¼ or less of the $/hr rate you charge the Customer, and you are giving your employees 30-40% of all labor revenue, the system usually works well, and employees make enough performance dollars to stay motivated.

The caveat to keeping a fixed rate for P4P, like 33%, is in the case that your team can't beat budgeted hours. This is especially apparent in seasonal businesses like lawn care. For example, when spring comes around at Augusta Lawn Care of Whatcom County in Bellingham, WA, we increase the percentage of labor revenue share to 40% for the months of March, April and May. This is because through this season our region experiences rain that ramps up alongside the rate of grass growth. This leads to more bagged clippings, slower mowing speeds, and more messy cleanup. Innately our teams move slower due to the condition, but we still want them to make above base pay. Again, if they don't feel like making performance dollars is possible, P4P will not change their behavior at all. The key to this shift is in its consistency and transparency, we make sure the team is aware that the percentage will increase for this time period and why it is increasing. We are sure to notify the date it will switch back to the 33%, and even give a reminder when the time is about here. No employee will ever complain if you increase this percentage, but be aware that your team will definitely have issues with a decrease. Clear communication and established policy allows us to adjust this percentage to match our industries needs.

This ties back to how the system is reliant on the owner to function properly. Creating this new culture of cooperation requires that you take the steps to ensure performance dollars are obtainable, as well as take the time to educate the crew on the standards, expectations, and calculations that are required for everything to run smoothly. While this doesn't mean taking it easy on your team, it does mean that you must have the ability to accurately budget jobs and allow a reasonable amount of time to complete the job. If your team isn't hitting above base pay, it is just as important to inspect your numbers as it is to look into their level of effort or efficiency. It can be an indication that your prices to the Customer are too low, or there aren't enough budgeted hours for a job. In the case of prices being too low, budgeted hours would be accurate and beatable but labor revenue too low for base pay to be eclipsed, even when budgeted hours are beat consistently.

P4P accentuates the good aspects of your business along with the bad, so creating an open dialogue with your team is important in fostering trust and growth in your company. Fostering that growth means maintaining work ethic and emphasizing quality of service. By setting the expectations and standards for the crew early on, they can operate within the rules of the game, and formulate strategies to win. Without predetermined regulations, the team can mistakenly prioritize speed and shortcuts over quality and efficiency. This is where your team will rely on you as the leader and referee to guide them on the right path, and maintain that balance. Having a brief and simple document that explains P4P and serves as the rulebook of the game is important. See Appendix A to see the two page document we use to explain P4P to our employees. We show this document during the hiring process and post it for all to see in our offices. The rules of the game must be known by all.

What will change for you?

Instead of micromanaging your crew, your goals should shift to gaining a firm grasp of the systems, and laying out clear guidelines for your team to follow. Knowing your numbers is the first step to this and echoes throughout this entire book. This means having an understanding of how the pay structure is implemented, and where the money is going but most importantly, having the skills and knowledge to share that information with your crew. Clear pertinent information directed to the individuals who need it will eliminate confusion, and ease the transition between hourly pay and Pay for Performance.

We look a lot at teams in this book, however it should be noted that this applies to businesses of any size. Whether you are a small business or running a large operation, these practices are applicable and relevant to smoothly transition to P4P. As a small business owner, you start to feel the strain of management the moment you grow beyond your first employee. The moment you can't be with each employee there is bound to be those questions of productivity and quality. P4P implemented in new or very small businesses may see less return in the short term. There may be times that P4P may not actually be beneficial for smaller companies. When a company has clients spread out around a wide geographical area and there is lots of drive time in a technician's day, it is unlikely they will be able to earn more than base pay, eliminating the positive potential of P4P. If your prices are lower to get started and have a 70%+ close ratio on your estimated proposals, you may also have a difficult time keeping labor revenue high enough for employees to make above base pay. If you are new to the business and cannot accurately predict budgeted hours on a job, I would also give a warning. At this point in the business I would recommend still implementing P4P, BUT be very open with your employees that you expect P4P to be a challenge to hit consistently. Let them know as time goes on, the business grows, prices are increased, and route density is improved, that they will make more money and make performance dollars more regularly.

When your business is operating at a smaller scale, you can see how with two employees you may only save four hours a day of wasted time, equating to something like $60 in net profit. To many, this may not be worth the extra strain of P4P implementation. But looking down the line as your company grows, the P4P system starts to exponentially increase in viability. A company with 15 employees might still only save two hours an employee, but that equates to $450 in net profit a day using the same ratios. Assuming 250 work days in the year that will lead to an additional $112,500 per year in pure profit!

If you are looking to stay small, maybe you and one other employee, P4P isn't for you. Hourly is simple enough to work in circumstances where the owner directly manages the employee, is on every job with them, and doesn't need the employee to work outside of earshot. But, if you are looking to grow your business, especially to the point where you step out of the daily operations, P4P is necessary to facilitate this growth. The earlier you adopt this method of compensation, the more waste you can eliminate from your business and the more sustainable your growth can become. You don't need to lose all your hair, ruin relationships, drain the bank dry, or go to a premature grave in the process of trying to scale your service business!

Chapter 5

Open Book Management

Open Book Management is imperative to running P4P effectively. With a new system of paying your employees there are bound to be questions and concerns. If the employees can't see what is happening behind the scenes, then they do not stand a chance at building a strong understanding of the system. The lack of understanding in the team will make it almost impossible to gain their trust, specifically because they can't put the pieces together themselves. The goal of P4P is to align the views of the employee and the employer. However, that isn't really possible if they don't have access to the same information. Working behind a veil of secrecy will only perpetuate their distrust and bolster whatever ideas, true or not, about your business. Opening the books is about taking a collaborative approach to business and breaking down the walls between "us" and "them" that hourly pay has so deeply instilled.

One of the biggest objections to opening the books is that the business is losing money, but this is actually the perfect scenario to implement open book management with your team. Showing them that the company isn't making money might scare some people, and will kick most into overdrive. Without open book management your employees will almost always assume you are making money hand over fist. They will look at indicators such as new equipment, more jobs, more employees to guess how well the business is doing. If the business is struggling, this is a perfect time to rally the troops and show them that you work hard every day and still make less money than they do every day. They will see your commitment to the business and unwavering belief that the hard work is going to pay off. They will respect the delayed gratification you are practicing and support you more. Open book management will start breaking down the walls forged by the "us" v.s. "them" mentality. This may be the biggest hurdle to implementing P4P, but is necessary for it to succeed since trust is a key ingredient.

Once you open your books, you suddenly open yourself up to scrutiny, and for some that pressure is what will prevent them from showing all the numbers to their Team. Owners may be afraid of the questions that will be asked by employees, and the fear that they won't know the answer. When starting out, it is a steep learning curve having to manage the work and the books, but as your business grows it is unsustainable to keep up the guessing game. You must know certain key metrics in your business on a daily, weekly, monthly, and annual basis. Once others' well-being depends on your ability to manage the business, it becomes even more pertinent to know your KPI's (Key Performance Indicators). That being said, if an employee asks a question about your company finances and you don't know the answer, just be honest and tell them you will check with your accountant and circle back with them.

If someone's livelihood depends on you getting the numbers right, then they should essentially be able to check your work. This redundancy enforces your accountability and reduces the risk for errors in your numbers. The conversation with an employee fixing a single discrepancy in the moment is much easier than months of errors causing distrust in the system. When you institute open book management you don't need to show ALL the numbers; however, I have consistently seen the most successful P4P implementations occur with the companies that have shown EVERYTHING in the books without hiding or masking anything. Why is this? Because the more transparent you are with your numbers the more the team will trust you, and that cannot be overemphasized on your journey to P4P paradise.

I recommend that you share how much you pay for rent, the cost of insurance, yes, EVERYTHING. Most employees have no idea of the expenses incurred to the business for things such as fuel, credit card processing, licensing, taxes, benefits, supplies and materials, software, legal and financial help, and the plethora of other line items on your chart of accounts.

How do you open the books?

It's not like there is an actual book sitting around with all the numbers neatly laid out in it, although that would be nice. It's a matter of sharing the concepts through real world examples with your team, and informing them on reports like your profit and loss statements. Show them what goes into a quote, and the hourly rate you're charging the customer. It involves explaining concepts like "customer acquisition cost" and "overhead recovery." Engaging your employees in the business will foster talent and promote growth. This is exactly why people seek internships; it's for the knowledge and experience they receive to then be applied in other areas, it's definitely not for the money!

Ask yourself: "how can I educate my employees so much that someone would intern at my business just to learn the numbers of the business, and how to cut out waste using P4P and open book management?" That question will change your mindset. It will get you past your fear of showing your prices and costs for everything in the business. Realize that P4P and open book management is a form of education for your employees, and this prevents an apple to apple comparison between you and the other 100 contractors in a tight labor market. You have intangible benefits in the form of education that cannot be weighed against, and do not compare to a difference in hourly wages. This education and learning is only valued by high performers, and will serve as a filter in your hiring process. I remember when I would do orientation for new hires at Augusta. I would tell them that the hourly wage and performance dollars they make would be good and significantly higher than our local competition; however, that was not the real long-term value of working at Augusta. It was that P4P showed them how to reduce waste and increase efficiency. That skill alone would set them up for great career prospects down the road. Open book management would unlock the knowledge of analyzing numbers and financial metrics, which would put them leagues ahead of any other applicants at future job openings.

When we first opened the books to the team, I went out and got $110.00 in one dollar bills. This was for the $1,100,000 of revenue from the previous year. Each $1 bill represented $10,000 in revenue. I assigned each employee an expense line item on the Profit and Loss Statement. One was rent, one was gas, one was insurance, another was repairs, one was credit card processing; and lastly, we had employee wages. Going down the list from our actual expenses, I handed "rent" $2, this meant that $20,000 was spent on rent the previous year. I handed out $5 to "repairs", and $4 to "gas", along with $4 to "credit card processing" and $2 to "insurance". There were a number of lesser line items, these totaled $19. I went all the way through the Profit and Loss statement and finally paused in front of the guy assigned "employee wages". At this point I had $84 left in my hand. I lay each dollar in "wages" hand one by one. In my hand, profits slowly dwindle; $65... $40... $25... $9 dollars left. As I stepped back and fanned my measly 9 dollars in profit, my team's jaws were on the floor. We were a decently busy company, and the team knew that, but to see just how little was left in profit was surprising at the least. Not to mention the fact that almost half of revenue went to one line item: employee wages. I held those remaining nine bills and said "this is the profit we work so hard for, and this is the money we will use to grow the business."

We explained that all the money we distributed were expenses and in each category waste was hiding. Our goal was to get this money back into profits, and distribute it back to the team. That night we sent the crew home with a task, to think about their assigned area of the business, and come up with ideas on how to cut out waste. "How do we get those dollar bills back into the profit pile?"

The next morning our assigned "gas" guy came back to the team, and proposed that the estimator for our lawn care business should drive a commuter car instead of a truck to save on gas. Another team member came up with the idea of storing fuel at the shop to reduce paying the highest price at the nearby gas station. Another recommendation was that a rag and spray bottle stay in each truck, and each day the crew was to wipe everything down. This would eliminate the need for someone to come in on the weekend and clean out the trucks. Another suggestion saved time and money on blade sharpening for the mowers. We all voted on the best cost-saving idea and the $110 in one dollar bills from the simulation was awarded to that individual. This planted the seed in our team's head to start thinking about the business as a whole, and to start thinking like the owner. This type of example might be useful in your company, since most front line employees will go cross-eyed if you pull pages of spreadsheets and numbers to view. This is a tangible way to see where the cash is spent in the business, and how important frugality and efficiency is to the growth of the business.

With all of the information behind the scenes, our front line workers were able to better assess the situation, and come up with creative solutions to improve the business as a whole. From that day on, we have created a space where employees no matter their position can actively voice their ideas, and make meaningful impacts on the company.

The Owners Income

Owners having worries about showing their own personal income is a common concern, however there are two ways to deal with this dilemma. Firstly, you can include your salary in the labor breakdown of your P&L. If you are an S-Corporation you should be paying yourself a reasonable wage/salary anyway. You work harder than anyone and should be considered part of the line item for wages. This inflates the labor cost, but keeps the profits realistic. If you are worried about having a massive profit number just raise your salary, which will effectively hide your actual income and reduce the bottom line.

The amount you actually take out of the business as a salary, is taxed, which encourages you to keep that number as low as possible to avoid losing a large portion to taxes, and then on the other hand you want to get enough out for yourself to support whatever lifestyle you'd like to live. These two pressures typically keep your salary to a reasonable amount and if you are struggling to find that amount, ask yourself:

"How much would it cost to hire someone to replace me to maintain profits?"

This number can vary based on your involvement in the business and can fluctuate based on your individual needs. This is a good rule of thumb on determining your part, and gives you a clear justification to your team on why you are getting paid that amount.

On the other side of the coin, you might be making "bank" as an owner. A viewpoint can be made, that as the owner you made the investment for years, and are now reaping the benefits. In this scenario the priority shifts from motivating the crew to save the business, to creating a path for them to get to where you are. Teaching them skills that transcend their current position, and propel them into a successful future, should become your priority as the owner. Opening your books will build trust that you're not trying to squeeze every dime out of your team, and show them you're trying to help them achieve bigger goals and dreams.

It comes back to turning everyone's focus to the same direction, and lifting each other up to achieve greatness. We have started the 3F Program at Augusta Lawn Care. This is short for the Franchise Fee Forgiveness Program. This allows any employee to become an owner without the cost of a franchise fee, after they work for 2 years on the front lines. When I have big profits I can say that we have opened up the books, taught P4P, and given them all the tools to get where I am at. I have blazed the trail and given them the necessary provisions to make it to the top of the mountain. The higher those profits the more inspired I hope they are to follow me into financial freedom using the newfound knowledge of waste reduction and understanding business metrics; all made possible by P4P and open book management.

Personally, I don't mind my Team knowing that I take a salary from the business, and what that amount is. If an employee ever questions that amount you would simply show them all the things that you currently do for the business. Marketing, hiring, accounting, sales, and the list goes on and on... You could attribute a "value" to each of these items and then simply stand back and say, "If you want more money, take these things off my plate and do them better than I can. Go for it!" With the first location of Augusta that now does $1.6-$1.8M per year in revenue. I don't mind my salary being low for tax purposes, but many times the profits are high. I make sure to give my Team a piece of those profits so they are incentivized to increase the bottom line, AND do not resent me for making a lot of money when I am not working at the business on a daily basis. We will talk about profit sharing in future chapters and how important it is if you are very profitable, but remain disconnected from daily operations.

If you are still hesitant on if open book management is something you should do for your business, reflect on why that is. If there is something you are trying to hide in your books, P4P probably isn't the system for you. This system is built on trust, and trust will inevitably be broken when hidden motives and spending are involved. Take this opportunity to visit current practices, and work towards improvement; whether that be hiring an accountant to sort your expenses, taking time to separate the business and personal purchases, or recalculating how you withdraw money from the business. These will more than likely be necessary for business success down the road, regardless. Open book management ensures that you get your Team culture into a position where P4P is easily implemented, and trust is fully integrated across the organizational hierarchy.

Chapter 6

The Transition

Building up to the actual transition from hourly pay to Pay for Performance can feel like a daunting task. Not only do you as the owner have to fully grasp the system, but you have to gain the buy-in from the team to adopt P4P. By breaking the process down into 3 steps, you'll have an actionable plan that has been tried and tested by companies all across the labor industry.

Step 1: Run the Numbers in the Background

During this stage you will calculate P4P on a daily basis, and start to run the numbers in the background to ensure you know what the base pay and % paid to the employee will be. Again, keep in mind during this step that you will see a 20-30% improvement in efficiency once P4P actually affects their paychecks. Presenting the Pay for Performance System to your team will be the first big step to transition. Do this at a Team meeting and print off the applicable policy document (example of Augusta's is in Appendix A) making appropriate changes and edits to your industry and business. Be prepared for questions. There will be tons! Addressing all of your employees' concerns ahead of time and laying out solid expectations will set you up for a smoother transition, in addition to setting groundwork for your culture to flourish. Keep in mind too, it is normal for employees to think that any change in their pay structure is

NOT in their best interest.

Lay out the clear timeline of the trial period from start to end. Schedule time to go over the full paycheck breakdown with each employee after the first and second check. Make sure it's clear what the expectations are for the job, and what could be at risk if not completed properly. Make clear the ownership they can take advantage of to go above and beyond during this trial.

Step 2: Two Paycheck Trial Period

Now comes the time to begin implementing your calculation in real time for your team. During the next two pay periods you will run a trial test on the P4P system, the caveat being that the team won't make any lower than they would make on their current hourly rate. This win-win scenario allows the team to get hands-on experience in the system without the risk of taking a hit on their compensation. There is no downside for them. They only have upside potential. It's important from your side to ensure this period is during a time of year that is reflective of the business overall, and where the team can actually make P4P. For instance, I would not have attempted this transition in winter, because this time of year is considerably more difficult to make a big P4P bonus with the outside factors. Take the time to teach them about the system and begin setting the standards for adapting this system.

Go over their Pay for Performance calculations for each day inside the pay period, and show them exactly what they made.

Teaching them the process and answering their questions is the most important part of building trust, and showing them the benefits of P4P. We run this trial for two pay periods (4 weeks), with the goal to have the entire team making above base pay by the end. Working with the crew after the first week to ensure the low performers are set up for success, is a preview of how things operate on this system. This trial period will indicate if your team will actually accept the new system. Obviously, if everyone just makes base pay, then no one will be looking to change the current system. However, your high performers are sure to excel when the ceiling is removed for them, and they can imagine their true earning potential.

Step 3: Vote on Implementation

This is where a vote comes into play as the final stage. Garnering the support of your team ensures the success of this system, so it is imperative that the majority of the team is on board for the switch. The choice being to either move forward with P4P or continue using hourly compensation. The outcome of the decision is permanent and there shouldn't be another trial period to be recalled later. As an owner it may seem difficult to relinquish this much control to your employees, however without their support the system will fail and gathering their input is another step towards building the battering ram of progress and ending the tug of war.

If you are confident in your numbers ahead of time and the majority of employees saw good performance dollars during the trial period, you shouldn't have friction in making the shift. However, you will soon see that low performers will hate the change. The hardest part is these might be employees who've gotten complacent over the years. As hard as it is, these individuals might leave your company or need to be fired. This sets the precedent for the team, and shows them not only the standards expected by you, but shows them that you won't let individuals hold back the team from improving themselves. You will be surprised that if 20% of your employees vote against the P4P system or leave your company, the remaining employees will increase productivity and you won't need to find new employees. This increased efficiency and output is what allows you to pay those remaining employees more money.

It's just as much about who you fire as who you hire.

As evil as this may seem from the outside, with the least productive employees getting cut with no remorse, it actually can be used as a helpful tool to build your team as a whole. Instead of holding company meetings addressing general issues that have come up, you now can see exactly where to allocate your time to improve the performance of the weakest link. Maybe the person hitting base pay needs more training or direction. Put that low performing employee for a few weeks with someone that is ultra efficient and crushes it on P4P. We've seen it time and time again where after working alongside a high performer, employees that used to be hitting base pay become some of our top paid workers. They just needed to learn, and the hourly pay system never tracked their efficiency or gave clear indicators of their weaknesses. Using the data that P4P provides can give you a new lens to view your business by allowing you the ability to get a better understanding of the health of your company as a whole.

A direct result of paychecks being intertwined with performance is the inherent self-policing of the crew. Your time spent micromanaging vanishes while their participation in improving the overall team dynamic flourishes. On an hourly basis a team member can ignore or "build a mental wall" to block out a lazy unproductive teammate, however on P4P if any part of the team is lagging behind it directly impacts their paycheck. This means that they will either develop the communication skills to deal with coworkers and train them to improve, or they will let you know that the employee is slacking. Low performers will be snuffed out from your business and unproductive employees taking naps or way too many breaks will last less than a day before other team members report them.

You now have the boots on the ground knowledge of how the team is working, and where improvements need to be made. There is no more hiring a person and waiting five or so weeks to see if they work out, your crew will let you know on the first day if they'll make the cut. Base pay will protect your Team from low performers or newbies that take too long learning but it will also incentivize them to incrementally train newcomers, and ensure the training is done efficiently while also remaining productive and getting work done.

A quick word of caution when raising the base rate. Similarly to the labor revenue percentage, base pay rate can't be lowered without major upheaval. You want the difference between their P4P and base pay to be as large as possible, because that will lead to the most money-motivated crew since the bulk of their pay will be based on performance and not guaranteed. I want the delta between low performers and high performers as high as possible; instituting an artificial base pay that is too high is the #1 way to demotivate your Team from really getting after it, and making lots of performance dollars. If base pay is too high, high performers will resent the fact that they only make a few dollars per hour more than the "lazy newbies". During the Covid pandemic of 2020 the labor market got VERY tight and it was hard to find employees. They were looking for secure, safe jobs during a very unstable time. To attract applicants, some of our Augusta locations had to raise their base pay past 25% of the rate we charged Customers. It was a short term fix that ended poorly for the culture and finances of these locations. This was fixed by lowering base pay or raising prices to the Customer to make the math work.

The Very First Transition

Only now can I look back and break down the transition in a three step process. We have done this successfully over 70 times at Augusta Lawn Care franchises and I have helped many home service businesses in various industries do it as well. When I first came to the conclusion to run this in my own business without this experience, it was like shooting blindfolded at a moving target.

Before the P4P implementation process, over dinner at a small joint in town, I was chatting with my managers about what it meant to them to be in the positions they are now, going over all they've learned and contributed over the years. I wanted their input on P4P. With sweaty palms, I knew that I would essentially be pitching to them, "What if I lowered the crew's guaranteed hourly pay but gave them a chance to make more sorta like a commission... maybe?"

At the time, I still didn't know if this thing worked. I knew at my core it would, but how to sell that to the people my business relied on was way over my head. It started with a simple sentence "What if we paid them all over $20.00/hr?" In my simulated numbers that was a low ball, but at the time I wanted everyone working in the field to have that earning potential.

Weak pitch aside, I had already opened the books up for my team and my managers knew I couldn't afford to pay anymore than I already was. Needless to say, they were confused. I explained that I had an idea that could make us all a ton more money by capitalizing on what we do best; innovate. Through innovating new solutions, we had already cut down on customer complaints, doubled the staff, and simplified our services. But I knew we could take it one step further. If we could scrub out those little imperfections that built up day after day, we could go from saving seconds; to minutes; to hours every day. But without the funds to pay the crew more to hussle every second of every day, I needed a system that could pass those savings between us.

So that's what I proposed, a two pay period trial phase to see if this crazy idea would work. The managers were hesitantly in, but then the real tricky part came. Pitching it to the crew.

During a morning meeting, I had set aside a little more time than usual to present this trial to the crew. I got a lot of side eye's, like they were saying I was off my rocker. There was a lot of skepticism, especially in my few crew members that were making $4-6/hour more than the proposed base pay. After diving deeper and answering so many questions, I saw hunger in their eyes and their drive was feeding the flame. We were ready for our trial.

After the trial period of two pay periods we were set to vote with the entire Team on whether or not P4P would be implemented. The day before the vote, I spoke to my managers and told them that I knew in my gut P4P was the best thing for the business and the employees. Even if the employees voted against it I told them I would probably use executive power to push it through. I knew in the long run it was the right thing to do! If that meant we lost all our employees, sobeit. P4P was going to happen!

In the end almost every single person was excited to commit to the transition. We had the vote. All votes submitted were in favor... but one.

Courage, Truth and a Side of Ketchup

As is customary by this point, we were holding the bi-annual team meeting offsite at a local burger joint. The whole crew was there, and we had plans to touch base, share exciting news, and go over the company expenses.

I stood and gave my speech to the team as they finished off their burgers and fries. It really wasn't anything out of the ordinary; we went over profits and goals for the new year, reflected on where we'd been and where we're going. As the end of the offsite meeting rolls around I always open up to any questions, and I mean anything. I think it's important as an owner to stand behind your business and take criticism, as well as hear out any ideas the team has to offer.

From the back of the room stood one of my more experienced employees, Bill. He had worked years and years in landscaping, and really knew his way around a project site. He was a wizard at hardscaping, and we all respected him for it. At this point he had been with us for over a year, and was one of our oldest and most experienced Team members. He was classic; his untied boots would clunk as he shuffled into the office every morning, a hot cup of coffee in hand, and would make his way on his route when he was good and ready.

We took extra care to make sure Bill was accommodated in employment with us. Vibrations from the weed eaters caused pain in his arms, so we made sure he had a full schedule of landscaping ready. During the winter, we brought him into the office to do some work and to get him out of the cold weather, and we always made sure he was heard with his grievances... even if they weren't always founded.

A good example of one grievance would be the Mercer landscaping project. We had scheduled it to start on a Wednesday, and had three crew members on it including Bill. He ended up getting in late that day, and when he found out the crew had left without him he was irate. He was claiming sabotage, and was furious they had taken "his" truck and "his" trailer. These were of course just company trucks and trailers, all of which are loaded up with the same tools and equipment. He had exclaimed that the team had purposefully left him the dirty trailer with all kinds of debris to clean, and he kept pulling the sabotage card. In reality, the crew took the truck and trailer that were assigned to them, and Bill would have been in that truck with them if he was here on time. It was very hard for my office staff to listen in. Thankfully, my office manager at the time graciously heard him out and talked him down through the whole outburst.

Unfortunately this wasn't uncommon for Bill. He had a consistent mindset that people were against him. We had hoped with the new P4P model however, that this would change this rut, encourage him to embrace the team and become a real key player.

The floor was now open for questions at the team dinner, and Bill came prepared. He had exclaimed, "This company is doing it WRONG!" What he said took me a moment to catch up to. He was calling me a cheat, a fraud; he was demanding raises, trucks, company phones; the whole nine yards. It was like poison, ranting about how terrible the business is, and how terrible I am as an owner. I was stunned. Just a few weeks ago I had taken him and his wife out to dinner and now to be standing here in front of my entire team, I didn't even know what to say. Some even joined in, adding comments here and there to push his claims.

His energy had crashed through the room, and left most of the crew frozen in panic and anxiety, with others looking at me expectantly for leadership and reassurance. I was so torn. On one hand, I'd love to provide things like personal trucks and work phones, things that were far out of the financial means of my small lawn care business. We had just gone over all of the numbers together, it was clear that was way off for us. Not to mention the personal stuff directed at me stung.

I was about to throw in the towel, say forget it to this whole P4P thing, open book management and profit sharing. I was done. I couldn't comprehend how I could give all I have to grow my team, look out for their personal success, and have them come back at me demanding the moon. But despite that, I stood there in the back of the burger joint and took it. I let everyone get out all their grievances. I let them voice their opinions and berate the company. I took responsibility for "misleading" them and didn't fight back. This was the point after all, the point of any questions. I wanted them to know that they were safe to have opinions to express themselves. I couldn't walk back on my duty to them to give them that liberty.

After that I got back to the studio and collapsed on my bean bag, I stared deep into the tiled ceiling wondering what it was all for? What was the point? I believed in my system and I believed in my company, so what went wrong? I couldn't sleep and I felt like I could barely move. I was literally in decision paralysis. Do I give up on this entrepreneurial dream or do I push forward? I knew I couldn't turn in the towel after five years of blood sweat and tears. I gave up medical school, my dream of being a surgeon, and a stable career... for what? To have my character questioned and my business picked apart by entitled and thankless employees? Maybe I made a mistake. Maybe I should have just stayed in school. Maybe I cared too much for my employees and was to blame for their entitled request for company phones and trucks when they knew that the business was barely profitable.

I started getting text messages. My team was reaching out, saying things like, "That was really rough, are you alright?", "It shouldn't have been said that way. That could have been handled much better", and even, "Please don't take what he said to heart, P4P has changed my life and I wouldn't want it any other way." This was fuel to my fire, and determination bubbled to the surface.

Between a rock and a hard place I decided to double down. I would work twice as hard to ensure my team knew everything about P4P. I would continue to improve the system, and make sure my team is behind it just as much as I am every step of the way.

So what happened to Bill? About a month or so later, everyone was getting ready to start their routes for the day. I had recently promoted a team member named Lee to be a new estimator. Lee was going around to all of the crews assigned to projects he'd bid; to make sure all of his job notes made sense and ensure he did a good job explaining what needed to be done. This was an initiative we greatly appreciated, and was one of the reasons we had chosen him for this position over some more experienced employees. Lee made it over to Bill's truck and asked the same question, "Do all of your job notes make sense, is there anything you're unsure of that I can clarify?" Bill turned around and barked at Lee, "No, I've been doing this for 15 years, I don't need your help!" At this moment, we knew he was not the asset to the team we needed him to be.

He was let go that day, because of the attitude that had been presented time and time again, but also to make a clear point to the rest of the team. It does not matter how experienced you are or how good you are at what you're doing, to treat anyone else on the team in such a way is not acceptable, and will not be tolerated. I made sure it was clear to the Team that he was fired for the way he spoke to Lee, not what was said a few weeks prior at the offsite meeting. I did not want them to think that they would ever be punished for bringing forward their ideas and constructive criticisms. Although I do not believe that Bill brought those ideas forward in a positive way and my pride wanted to fire him at the offsite meeting, I was glad that he was no longer on the Team and we could move forward with 100% buy-in for P4P.

Chapter 7

Efficiency Over Speed

One of the biggest concerns brought to the table by skeptical owners regarding Pay for Performance is losing quality standards. What is often heard when the team will move faster is that they are prioritizing speed and therefore will make more damages to client and company property and do a lower quality job with more mistakes which lead to more callbacks. P4P does not compensate for speed, it promotes efficiency. Being fast and being efficient are not the same thing. In reality, quality will actually be more prioritized over speed when looking at the definition of efficiency, from this perspective it is actually most efficient when tasks are done right the first time. If an employee is called back to a property or if a customer calls into the office with complaints, that is more waste than it would have taken for the job to be done right the first time. This is why we deploy systems like yellow slips, damages cases, and walkthroughs to ensure quality and bolster personal responsibility.

There are multiple levers you have as the business owner to maintain balance between speed and quality on the P4P system, and to uphold the standard of individual performance. **Manual Adjustments** being the umbrella term for these actions, they allow you to curtail the behavior of your team by having meaningful impacts on their paycheck. These come in the form of negative adjustments, such as damage cases; or positive adjustments, such as acquiring a new customer. WARNING: not understanding these manual adjustments clearly is what leads to most owners discounting or dismissing the idea of P4P, because they feel it takes away their control in the business. It does quite the opposite.

The Yellow Slip System

Yellow slips are your most powerful tool for ensuring quality and accountability in the workplace. The "yellow slip" system works in a five step process that addresses the issues, fixes it, then educates and empowers the crew. These are an opportunity to address problems that arise from daily operations, though not every mistake on a clients property requires a yellow slip. The biggest factor in determining the need for a yellow slip is to ask yourself, "Is there something to be learned from this?" If you believe that this employee or the team could learn a valuable lesson from the mistake, then that is when we'd initiate the yellow slip process.

The yellow slip process begins with a customer complaint or concern being submitted to the office. The manager or owner first confirms that there is cause for a yellow slip through either pictures or customer description. This is compared to the quoted service viewed alongside the previous standings with the customer. Taking into account the history of the customer can be a big determiner if further action needs to be taken. For example, if yellow slips are piling up on the property it could be the case that the estimate needs to be rewritten to better detail expectations to both the customer and team, or the customer may need to be let go if they are being unreasonable. Once there is a significant cause to assign a yellow slip, the physical yellow slip is created. This includes the client's name, clients address, date, the crew/employee that serviced, team/employee that will address the issue, description of the issue, and finally the resolution to the issue.

Date: 10/31/21

Territory: Coquitlam BC

Client Name, City & State: **Phillips, Zach**   123 Augusta Pl

Compaint or Issue:	Missed edging in the back yard by the dog run.

Resolution:	Return to complete edging.

Owned By: Mike Andes

Serviced By: Liz Naber

After the physical yellow slip is created it is vital to create a record in the employee's account detailing all of the information regarding the incident as well. This allows us to keep a log of previous interactions and find patterns in behavior to better train our team, and service properties with fewer mistakes in the future. This will also serve as a written copy of error in the case that the yellow slip turns into a fireable offense.

The next step would be following up with the team member. Likely we'll have them return to the property, by routing it into their schedule as soon as possible. This has saved our crew plenty of headaches in the field; all while maintaining our customer relationships. Having the employee return to the jobsite instills a sense of ownership for their work, but more importantly we also require them to try and contact the customer to go over the return visit. This bolsters their public relation skills, adds another layer of ownership to their work and will hopefully prevent another return visit.

Fig.2

Following the crew around fixing mistakes as the owner/manager disarms the crew, and monopolizes your time from being spent maintaining the business, not improving and growing it. If we are going to let them see the GOOD of P4P when they crush the budgeted hours on a job, we also need them to take responsibility for the BAD client complaints. Stop being reactive and spending half your day cleaning up after the mistakes of your employees. This disarms them from doing their job correctly and enables bad behavior. Also, on P4P when employees are making a percentage of the labor revenue, they will not want to be returning to a jobsite they have already been at. There is no new revenue being generated and therefore they don't get paid any extra to go back.

Once the issue is resolved, the Yellow Slip System has one final step to amplify the impact of return visits to the company. The employee who garnered the yellow slip talks about why they received the slip, what they did to address the issue, as well as identifying what the team can learn from it. They present this at the following team meeting with the point being to create that final sense of accountability, and to generate a learning experience for the whole crew. This is not a shaming exercise, but a way for the entire crew to learn from the mistake of one. There is even potential for an exchange of tips or training that can be shared from the team, to provide better service in the future. We don't want to embarrass anyone, but at the same time most employees dread speaking about their yellow slip with all their coworkers MORE than the deduction it creates on their P4P. At the end of the day you want this social pressure to make them take that extra few seconds to double check their work and prevent a callback. This leads to higher customer satisfaction since they actually care about the job being done right the first time!

It's only a mistake if nothing is learned from it.

The final presentation phase, and the implication to their performance dollars are the main drivers to avoid the slip in the first place. This effectively gives the overall ownership over each job as well as improves skills that are so often neglected in the labor field, such as public speaking. Employees who refuse to speak to the customer and do a walkthrough after a large project OR cannot address the team concerning their yellow slip, are let go. These individuals will not blend in to the culture of your business and are sure to create further upheaval down the line.

Implementing the Yellow Slip System to create learning opportunities for your crew, is the best way to make an impact on their daily performance and ensure quality. In the beginning it can feel overwhelming to address every new learning opportunity with a "slip," but as time goes on your team gets smarter and more diligent with their work. Yellow slips become far and few between as the team becomes a stronger unit overall, and they see the impact that callbacks and complaints have on their personal paycheck.

I had an employee named Watson that at the time was recently hired, and was on his 5th or 6th day mowing lawns by himself. It was a beautiful summer day without a cloud in the sky. While he was rounding the corner of the mailbox with the weed eater, a rock caught and flew into the front window of the house. It was a nice big window too, and it now had a smiling crack that stretched from either side. Not to mention, it was a customer's house that was notorious for nit picking our work. He had picked up his phone and rang Liz, our office manager immediately. "Liz, I hit the front window. There's a hole and a massive crack. I don't think the clients are home though."

Liz had cringed, but got to work contacting a few glass companies to see who could get the best rate and fastest turn around. She gave our customer a call and let them know the glass had broken and we already had quotes to get it repaired for them scheduled. They were incredibly pleased with our customer service, and were very thankful that we were already taking care of it. It wasn't something they had to come home and find out themselves.

Later that week during our team meeting, Watson

was sharing his yellow slip with the team. Everyone was very supportive, starting problem solving with him. One teammate had said, "Did you keep your back to the house?" another asked, "Did you do a sweep for rocks beforehand?" They would debate if these solutions were time efficient, and how this can improve their overall service of a property. It was incredible. I watched with pride as my team stepped up to the plate together and came up with better ways to work moving forward, and avoid another broken window. A yellow slip is created ANYTIME that a damage case like this broken window happens. Yellow slips are also created for any callback from an unhappy customer. Yellow slips are your ticket out of being the quality control person for all your employees. It makes them accountable to each other, the business, and the Customer... ultimately being tied to their paycheck.

Manual Adjustments

When a situation happens like this particular window incident, how does this relate to their P4P? Thankfully since we are on a biweekly pay schedule, things like this are usually fully covered by an employee's performance dollars for that paycheck. If the cost of repair is greater than their performance dollars, the remaining cost of repair does NOT come out of their base pay. This extra cost to the business still affects the employee since it ultimately reduces profits, which later down the line affects the entire team if you choose to do "profit sharing." An important note to take away: on P4P, performance dollars is the only part of a paycheck that you are able to make adjustments on. Remember, performance dollars is the bonus earned in excess of base pay plus overtime. Furthermore, that manual adjustment should only be done for a current paycheck, never past or future paychecks.

It is illegal to take away from the hourly wage or base pay of an employee, at any time. ONLY THE BONUS is on the table if an employee gets yellow slips. I do not recommend taking away performance dollars from multiple pay periods. For example, let's assume someone damages a Customers fence while mowing their yard. The cost of replacement from a local contractor is $420. You also deduct one hour of time for the office to coordinate the fence repair, a cost of $50. The total cost of the yellow slip is $470. However, at the end of the pay period this employee only has $200 of performance dollars. In this case we would take off that $200 on this paycheck, but no more deductions for this incident will occur. You do not want that employee showing up the following pay period KNOWING that there is no way for them to make above base pay. They will go slow and drag down the entire Team that is still trying to perform at a high level. The $200 loss is pain enough for that employee to learn their lesson and be more careful around fences in the future.

Before taking an adjustment from someone's P4P bonus regarding broken tools and equipment or company property, it's important to decipher if this was a negligent incident, or if it was equipment failure. For example, a crew member backs their truck over a wheelbarrow, and it breaks the wheelbarrow. That will be removed from their performance dollars, because they neglected to check their surroundings before driving. Say a crew member is using a rake to spread soil, and the rake snaps suddenly, that will NOT be taken from their P4P bonus. The crew member was using the equipment properly and the equipment failed.

This prompts the question of "damage pools", a predetermined fund that is taken from any time a damage case arises. Some owners will just announce to their team at the beginning of the year, "Okay, so we have $10,000 in the damage pool. Every time there is a damage case we will pay for it out of this pool of money. Anything left over will go to the Team at the end of the year." Sounds great, right? No. This "end of year bonus" is usually too far away to change the behavior or performance of entry-level employees TODAY. They will only care about that year-end bonus when December rolls around, and only IF there is still money in that damage pool. The P4P method of adjustments incentivizes employees to take true ownership of a damage/loss mistake, and make the effort on their own to improve and do better in the future. The damage pool is also flawed with deciding how much will be in the fund.

There is absolutely no way of knowing how much damage there will be in any given period in time, and doesn't explain why the entire Team gets penalized for the mistakes of one individual. The goal of P4P is to get the incentive (bonus) as close to the performance as possible. Annual bonuses rarely motivate an employee to run across the parking lot, instead of walking, or cut out their 5th gas station stop of the day. DAILY reporting of P4P and the direct impact it has on their paycheck TODAY will motivate and inspire the Team to think differently now. Money talks!

In the case of Watson's broken window from before, this played out a little different. Even though he was newer, he was already taking extreme ownership. He felt so dejected, and was determined to make up for it. Besides his mowing routes for that week, he was also scheduled for a landscaping project that Friday, that would inevitably roll over into the next pay period the next week. As we will discuss soon, multi-day projects are paid out in P4P dollars only after the full project is completed. Watson took this into consideration with the cost of the window (it ended up costing around $600.00), and he knew that if he finished that landscaping project he would have enough P4P to cover the full cost. So with the customer's permission, he set up a spotlight and continued working late past his shift. This type of accountability can only come when the employee knows, understands, and feels the pain from their mistakes.

The office manager was getting alerts on her phone from the security cameras, it was around 10:30 at night. She looks at the footage and sees Watson, knowing he wanted to work later she assumed he was dumping the debris or something before heading home. She then got another notification at 1:00 AM, when he was just rolling back into the shop with his equipment. Liz called him, and asked what he was doing at this hour still at the shop. She recalled him saying, "I wanted to make up for what I did. My P4P wasn't going to cover the full cost of that window, and I wanted to make sure it did." So in this special case, we decided he would not pay for that whole window out of P4P dollars, he would only pay half. For him to go out of his way and show that kind of integrity and determination was inimaginable, we could not let that go unnoticed. However, we did make clear that we can't work at a customer's property at night, with a healthy dose of teasing.

Along with performance dollars the damages may also affect the profit sharing if your company is to that stage of development. This isn't a punishment directed by the owner at their employees but is an unfortunate repercussion of paying for damages, thereby lowering the overall profits. The effect this has on the team is a unification of fault, for example when Augusta had over $5,600.00 in trimmers stolen it took about $50.00 from everyone's profit sharing that quarter to replace them. This turned the situation from "They stole from Augusta" to "They stole from us", uniting the crew to ensure their equipment was locked up every night and to brainstorm solutions to better secure our facility. As the operations manager, your job is to ensure the work gets done well and that each member is performing to the best of their ability. These methods of damage recovery as well as quality enforcement, allow you to conduct a better business while making meaningful impacts on the actions of your crew.

What if a return visit is needed, and the employee liable is not available? Typically with a yellow slip, the guilty team member returns to the job that they made a mistake on. This is the easiest way to calculate P4P since no manual adjustments are needed. The crew member simply returns to the job, fixes the issues and continues their route. This will inherently impact their P4P for that pay period, since it will reduce their earning power on the day they return to the jobsite. However, in this case a different team member would be sent over to fix their mistake, and they are paid by the hour for time spent on the property, which then comes out of the P4P from the employee that made the error. In terms of adjustments: a negative dollar amount adjustment is added to the employee who made the error, and the employee fixing the error will be working at base pay rate during this time. This is good for two reasons. First, the guilty Team member usually thinks they can make the repair/resolution the fastest and therefore do not want others taking their yellow slips. Second, the person that returns to do the job won't be very happy with the person that made the mistakes since being at base pay for that time takes away their ability to make performance dollars on another job. Again, this enforces accountability and removes the burden placed on the business to clean up after the team.

Walkthroughs

A call back to the office is one of the largest unnoticed inefficiencies of running service based businesses. Typically this means taking time from one of your highest paid non revenue producing employees and allocating it to resolving issues from a third person perspective. This is common in the lawn care industry as some customers have a higher expectation of service than agreed upon. Although we do deduct the time of office employees from the P4P of an employee that has a yellow slip, we do want to avoid these callbacks as much as possible. We have implemented a simple, yet effective solution for dealing with this which was proposed by our team on the P4P system.

A simple walkthrough after the work has been completed has proven to nearly eliminate the call backs we receive at our office. This policy has had a substantial impact on the company as a whole, and is another example of the ingenuity generated in the P4P system. Once a project is nearing completion; meaning all of the tools are still readily available and cleaning up has not yet been done, the crew member asks to walk over the job with the customer to essentially check their work. This not only builds the communication skills of the employee but allows them the opportunity to adjust any preferences or details before they leave. This can include trimming back a bush another inch, pulling a small plant they see as a weed, or one of the bricks edging the garden is a little crooked. These are things that would have cost the business in waste, or in the employee perspective, P4P time having to drive back the next day to resolve such a small qualm for the customer.

Walkthroughs make the customer feel heard and give a sense of ownership if they do need to call in later.

Instead of receiving a call from an irate customer the call is much more civil and any issues can typically be resolved on the following service instead of having to schedule a return trim. Such a powerful solution to a complex issue couldn't have been conceived on an hourly system, because the parties involved are so detached from one another. Shy employees that are not used to confrontation or speaking to strangers will usually forego the walkthrough once they have completed a project. However with P4P, this has a direct impact on the paycheck of the crew on-site, and they realize that 5 minutes of discomfort doing the walkthrough is better than a yellow slip, returning to appease an irate customer, and then publicly talking about that mistake in front of the Team. P4P unites your team and fuels their ability to problem solve, eliminating inefficiencies throughout the entire business.

Another contribution walkthroughs provide is grounds to upsell the customer on other services the employee may have noticed while working. The ability to sell is the beating heart of business, and if an employee can gain those skills in the field their potential to achieve their future vocational and financial goals is exponentially greater. An example of this is while servicing weeds in the garden beds, the employee noticed a few dead limbs on a tree that would look much better cut off. This upsell can often take the form of property clean ups and bush trimming as well. When they manage to upsell a customer we make manual adjustments to their performance dollars; for our team if they upsell an existing customer they'd be given a $10 bonus, but if they sell a new customer it is a $50 bonus. This amount we give them is equivalent or less than our CAC or our "Customer Acquisition Cost" that we would usually pay to Facebook, Google, or the USPS for a print marketing campaign. I would rather give those marketing dollars directly to my Team and incentivize the employees to be on the lookout for new work.

Using these tools to ensure the quality of the work is maintained is just as important as getting the work done in the first place, that is why the focus must be placed on efficiency. The affiliation between speed and efficiency is apparent. However, highlighting the waste generated from customer complaints with the time allotted to resolving these issues, strengthens the employees ability to prevent such issues from arising. I encourage you to use words such as productivity and efficiency over emphasizing SPEED when talking to employees about P4P.

The advantage of P4P is getting employees to think like owners, and that starts with educating them on the full picture of running a business with the impact they have within the company. Giving them the power to fix their mistakes and the opportunity to learn skills beyond the physical labor associated with the work, will motivate them to keep improving. Shifting the perspective from "What is my employee doing wrong?" to "How can I give them the tools to cut waste and improve themselves?" will inevitably improve the company as a whole.

Chapter 8

Understanding P4P

Pay for Performance is a new method of compensation. With change there will be an abundance of questions, misconceptions, and doubt. Change, time and time again, is feared in our society, and the solution to this hesitancy is education. Looking from a bird's eye view at the common misconceptions of P4P, we can address controversial topics like overtime, project pay, and skill based bonuses to provide clarity for you and your team. Taking the time to understand these pain points equips you with the tools to firmly justify your actions, allowing you to educate your team on the procedures, and set proper expectations for their pay structure. P4P highlights the importance of building a team of collaborative members. Each person will have the knowledge to generate helpful feedback and to understand Pay for Performance.

Building trust and understanding takes time, and this can be one of the hardest things you'll overcome as an owner. After we had implemented P4P, I started to hit these same bumps in the road. Without the knowledge I now have those bumps turned into massive hurdles that usually ended with collateral damage of unhappy employees, dissatisfied Customers, and unprofitable work. I hope you can learn from my mistakes and implement P4P in a way that circumnavigates these hurdles.

Overtime

In P4P, we incentivize efficiency and promote cutting waste. To a business, overtime is considered waste, as it is a higher labor cost that ultimately does not equate to higher production. Overtime tends to build up especially in season dependent businesses, and it can be confusing for a team working longer hours that is seeing less returns on their P4P dollars. The fact of the matter is that overtime is a form of waste and that is exactly what P4P is designed to eliminate. The team doesn't accrue more performance dollars in overtime. Remember, we calculate base pay versus P4P earned over the course of the entire pay period. To further break it down, Base Pay + Overtime Pay VERSUS P4P + adjustments means that in the case of excessive OT, the crew will notice they are making closer if not exactly the same as base pay.

One argument is that they are working overtime and thus deserve P4P on top of that, however overtime costs the business and the point of this system is to eliminate costs and pass the savings onto the crew. With no savings to be had, the business has nothing to share with the employees. The conversations we've had with our employees around this subject build on the fact that we can absolutely bring on new team members to cut out overtime. The trade off is that in the slow season, there isn't enough work for everyone to see massive profits. In the end it really depends on your team, if they want more employees to alleviate the load, then it is your responsibility as the owner to increase your crew or decrease your work; however when things slow down you may find yourself having to cut people to remain profitable. The crew is more likely to stick with it during overtime regardless of the P4P implications if they understand that hiring more employees to alleviate the short term work spike, will result in them making less money during the slower months.

Although this pain point can seem infuriating to most at first, it is an unfortunate cost of inefficiencies in the business. The reason the employees are upset is the same reason the owner is, with the accelerated workload there isn't enough labor revenue to cover the budgeted hours. This causes strain on the business and because Pay for Performance better aligns the owner and employee perspective, they both feel the stress of the overload; where hourly the owner is the only party who takes the hit. Trust me, on hourly pay, the employees know the exact minute they are in overtime and making time and a half. Using the P4P system, the employees know that moment as well, and do their best to get their work done beforehand since the returns after that point diminish. We've had innovative solutions birthed from this tension by our team in the past, such as hiring a separate person to clean the shop, trucks, and equipment on the weekend. This alleviates the overtime generated from the team sticking around after their shift to do this maintenance themselves. In this case we were able to address one source of overtime and cut waste, passing the savings back to the team.

Multi Day Projects & Positive Adjustments

For typical work, P4P is calculated daily and is accumulated throughout that time period. Things get a bit more complicated when a project is scheduled to take multiple days, because performance dollars can't be calculated until the job is completed. This is simply because it's impossible to know what percentage of the performance dollars goes to each person involved until we have all the data regarding a job; in particular, how long it actually takes. Even with one person on the job, you can't be sure that by the end of it another person won't be involved in its completion.

If the job starts and finishes within the pay period then this isn't an issue. The performance pay will accumulate like any other job once finished. A situation is bound to arise however where a job crosses between two or more pay periods, this is the point where red flags are raised and a bit more thought is necessary. In these cases the employee will be paid out at base for their hours worked, but the performance pay for that project won't be applied until its completion. This doesn't mean withholding all the performance dollars from that pay period, rather it means the employee is more likely to hit base. It's important to make a distinction between one-day jobs or routes, and multi-day projects, so that the time allocated is appropriately accounted for, and applied to the right paychecks once it's done. This is one reason why I recommend a two week pay period on P4P. This allows larger jobs to be completed within a single pay period without having to withhold performance dollars on a job that the crew is crushing. If you commonly have jobs that take months on end to complete, you could create checkpoints throughout the project that could allow for P4P to be run more consistently. Breaking a massive project into smaller line items on the estimate would allow you to have specified amounts of budgeted hours allocated to parts of the job, making it easier to break apart and run P4P on throughout the project timeline.

Projects also offer a form of upward mobility for your team. At Augusta, any project that exceeds 48 hours requires a project manager. We use 48 budgeted hours because that is the equivalent of 3 days of work if 2 people are assigned to the job. This project manager person is involved in overseeing the project, everything from communicating to the client to being responsible for its completion. They will work with the team to ensure everything runs smoothly, and will be the line of communication to the office and keep information organized. They are usually the employee that will ensure materials are loaded, rental equipment secured, and the truck ready to roll out each day of the project.

This team member is typically the most experienced team member, however in some circumstances if there are multiple experienced employees on the job they can share these responsibilities. To incentivize our team to ensure quality and efficiency in experienced positions, we add "project management" bonuses to their P4P dollars. In our case this is a $1.50/ budgeted hour increase on top of their project P4P. The reason this bonus is applied to their P4P and not base pay, is to continue to incentivize their efficiency on the job, and to ensure they receive the benefits of their leadership skills. For example, if there was a job with 100 BH (budgeted hours) and 3 people were assigned to it, that would mean that $150 would be set aside for a project management bonus at the end of the job. Let's assume that the crew gets the job done in 90 actual/clocked hours. Each employee worked 30 hours on the project. If one of the employees did all the tasks associated with project management that individual would receive a $150 bonus, the equivalent of $5/hr more than their peers. This is a way to retain employees with lots of experience and skills. This way on high-skilled jobs the grunt laborer is not necessarily making as much as the person that has machine operation training or industry-specific experience. In the event that more than one employee split the role of project manager, the $150 bonus could be divided however the manager/owner seems fit. If your business focuses primarily on high-skilled labor, you may want to consider raising the hourly project management bonus to $3/hr or more.

Training a new employee can be time consuming, and can hurt the trainers' Pay for Performance dollars having to slow down and explain/teach things. To counteract this, we have a training "manual adjustment." This is a $4.00/hr bonus, calculated with the length of the shift and added to the P4P bonus. This is to encourage experienced team members that are training, to do so efficiently and thoroughly while on the job. Though it is calculated differently than the project manager bonus, they both ensure quality of work and fairness when having unequal levels of skill present on a crew.

In lawn care this would look like an experienced member taking out the newbie on their mow route, and feeding them larger and larger tasks to train on, while the lead member is actually completing the route as they go. In order to remain productive the trainer would start with simple tasks such as edging and using the blower, and slowly build on those skills as the trainee becomes proficient at those new tasks. Maybe on day two they show them how to use the push mower. On day three the zero turn is used. Day 5 might consist of training on how to back up the trailer or using a skid steer. This incremental training process cuts down the waste of long and elaborate training sessions that don't focus on getting employees to a profitable level of proficiency as soon as possible. This way of training also reduces the financial strain of bringing on new crew members, in an industry that has notoriously high turnover. These positive adjustments are typically called for in cases of experienced labor as well. Work outside the typical scope of your team that can pose an increased danger to the employee, are good times to enact these sorts of manual adjustments. This allows your team to breathe easier while prioritizing safety and quality in these situations. Skill based bonuses offer tangible incentive for upward mobility in your company as well. This gives experienced employees a path to continuously earn more by removing the plateau of their efficiency by allowing them to focus on building a large portfolio of applicable skills to better help the business. Keeping these bonuses tied to budgeted hours is much more ideal since you still want efficiency to be the goal and not racking up clocked hours.

Contracts

When our business grows and we earn a positive reputation, there is a potential for commercial and association-type work. Typically with these kinds of customers, they will ask to have a flat rate and a range of services to be taken care of. These usually take the form of a contract; the customer pays a set rate each month for the year, and we provide an umbrella of services throughout that time frame. When considering P4P, and even more importantly correctly bidding on the full scope of work, it is important to not only lay the groundwork or what services will be done, but the specific schedule of these services ahead of time. Every single service and visit must have accurate notes and budgeted hours associated with it.

Take for example an HOA that wants to have mowing, weeding, bed maintenance, and tree/bush trimming all enveloped in a contracted rate. Using your knowledge of the growing seasons, grass types, and climate you predetermine the frequencies of these services. At Augusta, we have a template on hand to help determine these factors. Here's an example of how we would fill this out. Keeping mind that the dollar amount shown has been calculated based on budgeted hours multiplied by the hourly rate for that service:

---

12 MONTH CONTRACT:

1.) Mowing:
    a. Weekly Visits March-June / Sept.-Nov.
    b. Bi-Weekly Visits July-August
    c. Includes Knocking Down Grass on Hillside Along First Street
    d. Includes All Other Lawn Areas
(($140 (weekly price) x 26 (visits)
+ 210 (biweekly price) x 8 (visits) = $5,320))

2.) Weeding:
    a. Bi-Weekly Visits March-Nov.
    b. Pull Large Weeds in Garden Beds
    c. Remove Garbage and Debris
    d. Spray Areas of Heavy Weed Growth
    e. Blow Off Parking Lots
(($300 spray + $90 (biweekly price) x 20 (visits) = $2,100))

3.) Tree and Bush Trimming:
    a. To be Completed in March, August and November
    b. Trim and Shape Bushes lining Walkways and Driveway
    c. Trim Any Low Hanging Branches from Magnolias
    d. Trim Bushes or Trees That Are Touching the Siding of Homes to Reduce Algae/Rodents
    e. Haul Away Work Related Debris
    f. Video Recorded for Service Crew
(($420 (Per Visit) x 3 (visits) = $1,260))

(($8,680 TOTAL / 12 Months = $723.33))

    The biggest issue I see when contract work has been accepted, are factors left to the employees interpretation for service. Say a service visit includes weeding the flowerbeds and the job notes say to "pull weeds as needed."

 Fig.3

If we have one employee who skips weeding for 3 weeks, because they don't think it is "needed" there might be an exorbitant amount of work the next time we are there to service, or the client will complain. You do not want to leave anything up to subjective standards or leave room for ambiguity in a contract. It's best to lay out the expected timeframe of every service for the year, compile the overall price to the client, and then lay out the expectations for the employee using the job notes on every single visit. Laying out the frequencies ahead of time ensures that there is no gap in the agreed to service, but also gives an accurate budgeted hour for these services throughout the year to calculate P4P accurately.

This is why on P4Psoftware.com we have the Advanced vs Simple use of running P4P. You will need to use the advanced method if you have contracts. The reason for this is on contracts, you have level monthly billing and yet the amount of work required on a given month varies dramatically. That is why allocating budgeted hours for every service and knowing the frequency of that service is vital to running P4P correctly. This practice is also useful for making sure that your estimate proposal on these large contracts are accurate and retain good profit margins. This means that if the client ever complains about the grass being "too tall" during July, you can simply present the contract that clearly states the frequency during that month and the option to increase that frequency at a given price based on BH.

Know When to Use P4P

As we've explored in this book, P4P is a tool that gives the employee power to increase their efficiency to earn more. These opportunities take form in tasks we do often, and can continually work to improve on. As is the case for lawn care, these services may not go year round as lawns go dormant and do not need mowed. To fill this gap in work, we can take things on like Winter Services, where we spend the same amount of budgeted time as a biweekly mow on a property to clean up any debris, inspect for issues and keep lawns looking great through the off season. This can also be hanging holiday lights, and snow removal services.

In terms of these services, we do not give the P4P incentive. When guaranteeing an amount of time, we cannot expect our team to finish early, therefore earning P4P. In the case of hanging lights and snow removal, these are simply too dangerous and risky to incentivise anything other than taking time to do it correctly and safely. If a high performer is looking to make high P4P dollars plowing snow and hits a car, not only does that hit the employees profits, but it is a much more substantial cost to the business. If an employee falls while hanging lights at a property, the medical expense is too high to justify any profit from speed.

When taking these factors into consideration, they may not be worth doing the service in the first place. Take into consideration the cost to acquire the equipment for these sorts of tasks and the liability costs to complete it, these might not be worth your time. This is the exact reason why I've implemented a height limit for tree trimming services at my shop. The risk of injury or damage from a high up falling tree limb is not worth the possible profit for these services, let alone the commercial insurance cost triples as well.

Growth Beyond the Front Line

Building a path for your employees to strive for eludes to a maturing business, where the owner has pivoted priorities from growth to sustainable earnings. When it becomes apparent to the employees they bring value to the company, and they can reach and exceed personal goals, your business will foster the long term retention of talent. By tradition, in an hourly model this path is predictable, and typically looks like incremental increases beyond hourly and into salary. For some positions, though, this business model works fine, as by this point the employees are finding gratification through the work and not purely through the monetary incentives. This can be found in creative jobs such as videography, media production, art, and music where measuring performance is far more subjective, budgeted hours in this case is a poor use of productivity.

However, on the P4P system the path beyond front line workers seems less clear. This poses a question that with factors such as age brings: Will the employee reach a plateau where eventually they can't keep up with the pace, and slowly drop off? The solution to this question is baked into the nature of P4P itself. The culture built around this system is designed to build an individual's skills beyond the labor market, and prompts them to expand their knowledge to all aspects of the business. This personal growth gives them the tools they need to go beyond the physical side of the labor market and expand into administrative, leadership, or management positions, or becoming an owner themselves.

At Augusta we have gone even further by creating paths like the "3F Program" to lay the groundwork for exactly this. The "Franchise Fee Forgiveness Program" allows any employee from Augusta to start a franchise location for no startup fee, saving $25,000, after working for the company for two years. These pathways to building a future for everyday employees is what fosters long term relationships and for many is the motivation that pushes them to exceed expectations on the P4P system.

It's not everyday you stumble across pure talent bursting at the seams, but of course when you do it seems to be when you don't need it. The story of when I met Lee was no different. My Office Manager, Liz, had come to me bright eyed and excited. She told me about a Moody Bible Institute graduate working at the local Parks and Recreation campground who had stopped by the shop, looking for an employment opportunity. We were going into the winter season, and I sure didn't need some smart guy with a degree in theology coming into our industry with no experience, right when we slowed down for the year. Liz was convinced that I needed to talk to him and I had learned to follow her intuition when it came to HR. Sure enough he came in for an interview and he was solid, he really knew his stuff and could talk his way out of anything. So we offered him a job, and started problem solving ways to keep the crew busy for the season.

Lee was this mystery gent that turned out to be perfectly suited to destroy our numbers on P4P. He caught on fast. He was out there everyday tweaking his route and strategizing with the crew to find just the right way of mowing stripes all across Bellingham. The team liked him, we liked him, and the customers loved him, so naturally he moved into the role of the estimator; and man did he know how to sell. We were getting so busy thanks to him shouting the name Augusta from the rooftops that we could barely keep up. He was hungry to learn, grow and expand and within Augusta we had built a culture that fostered that. Through open book management he learned how we ran the business and through P4P he learned how to better estimate jobs. Lee was going places and everyone knew it.

After a few years of working in the office as Operation Manager, Liz moved on to the franchise side of things and running our Command Center. Lee stepped in full time running the daily operations at the local shop. He was our first employee to go through the entirety of the P4P system and rise to the top as a leader. His hands-on experience from working in the field earning P4P himself gave him the ability to address the crew's concerns on a personal level. He was able to allocate resources and manpower with the same mentality that Pay for Performance had instilled in him, allowing the team to be as efficient as possible. Thanks to systems like profit sharing, he was still just as connected as ever to the business and the crew knew it. It's not everyday you come across an all-star, but setting up a pathway for individuals within your company to grow is what this system is all about. If you are concerned about higher skilled or older employees struggling with a performance based pay system, know that the growth that will come to your business as a result of P4P will usually lead to a need for higher paid leadership positions that these individuals can fill.

Therefore, open book management becomes more pertinent as time goes on, as you're bound to run into friction around aspects like pricing jobs. In order for the employees to be able to run P4P in their heads they have to know at least labor revenue for the job. However, in most jobs the labor revenue isn't the entirety of the cost to the customer. For example if your team is in the field getting 33% percent of a sod install which you've told them has 20 budgeted hours at $80/hr then they are under the impression that the job is $1,600. As the owner/estimator you know that isn't the case, in reality the job is $2,470.00 after the dump fees, material costs, and delivery costs. This situation can set up the owner in a position to be perceived as stealing from the team by "lowering" the total of their P4P earnings. Without being educated on the costs inherited with the job, the team can only assume you are skimming the $870 difference off the top.

Opening up about the nuances of pricing a job and what each piece entails for the company is the framework that sets up employees to expand their understanding of the field beyond the physical work. Having this knowledge empowers the employees to make more accurate decisions on the job site as well as providing another perspective on improving efficiencies throughout the business as a whole. Paying attention to pain points, and addressing them is taking the preemptive steps to ensure P4P will run smoothly after the transition.

Building a foundation of trust through transparency with your team you foster the collaborative culture that the system thrives in. This bolsters the skills of each team member, improving their value to the company, boosting their personal returns on P4P, and upgrading their future earning potential by changing their mindset. All of this growth allows you to lay the groundwork for upward mobility, ensuring the long term retention of these employees. Improving the dynamic between the employee and the employer through this objective system, where the entire team is responsible for the successes and failures of the business. It devillainises the owner and allows them to become a referee; by making the calls based on the rules and not their subjective feelings.

Chapter 9

Calculating P4P

For many of us, we are working long days out in the field and hate nothing more than coming home, and having to sit in front of the computer doing the office work. This is exactly how I felt pouring over the numbers late into the night, in my poorly lit office pondering if P4P was the right move. I simply couldn't have the calculations take longer than the time saved. That's why I built P4P off of this moto:

One Minute, Per Employee, Per Day.

I needed it to become this fast in order to make switching worth it, and I knew with each employee the process becomes exponentially harder. This is what fueled my drive to create spreadsheets, web apps and eventually *P4Psoftware.com*; all to propel Pay for Performance to where it is now. We'll look at what it takes to crunch the numbers; the reason why most owners will never make the switch to P4P!

Hourly is such a simple calculation and that's the reason it has become the standard. Even with its simplicity there are still gray areas like drive times, commutes, and breaks. Do you pay your employees when they are driving to their first job? Do you pay them for lunch breaks? What if they need to take a 15 minute personal call? P4P isn't a perfect system either, but it does far more for the employee and employer while keeping its roots in this same simplicity. Based on two calculations, we run the numbers to find the wages for each employee each day. The first of which is their base pay, this is the floor of their potential earnings and is their pay as if they worked hourly.

Base Pay Wages = (Hours worked x Base Pay) + (Overtime Pay x Over Time Hours)

This number is run against their performance dollar total at the end of the pay period, to ensure they won't make less than a certain amount. The performance dollar total, or their P4P, is determined similarly.

P4P = (Total Labor Revenue x P4P Percentage) +/- Manual Adjustments

These two totals are summed up at the end of each day for each employee. I recommend this daily frequency to eliminate errors when applying adjustments and determining where everyone spent their time on the clock. Although they are run everyday, the higher of the two summation isn't taken till the end of the pay period, where all the totals for each side are added up and compared. This daily approach is akin to keeping a finger on the pulse of your business. It indicates it's overall health, allowing you to make more educated decisions as the owner.

All roads lead to payday, when what's paid out and how it's notated is all put together by you. Building out a reliable pay schedule, ensuring employees are being fairly compensated and getting all ducks in a row on the back end is just as important as any other aspect of business. Scheduling a pay period that you can reliably meet, and which employees can sustainably live off of is the tightrope that we walk. The typical pay period is a bi-weekly or every other week, and that system integrates with P4P perfectly.

Two weeks allows for yellow slips and other manual adjustments to be accurately applied to performance dollars. On a weekly or daily payout frequency, the likelihood of these instances popping up after the applicable pay period becomes more and more common. The importance of having the ability to apply adjustments timely, becomes apparent when an employee rushes through their work leaving a trail of yellow slips in their wake. If you can't take the performance dollars generated from their rushed work then there might not be any to take from their future work. Furthermore, taking money from subsequent pay periods, say in the event of damage cases, demoralizes an employee and kills their drive to perform in the first place. This is the case when considering project work. Projects that take multiple days need to be completed before the P4P can be allocated, and two weeks allows for most projects to be wrapped up and calculated before the pay period deadline. By having a longer pay period, you also allow potential performance dollars to accumulate. This becomes an even greater incentive to be careful to avoid damage cases and yellow slips, since the amount the employee could lose increases.

Looking to extend to a monthly pay schedule and encompass more multi day project work, typically doesn't work for the employees. Typically, this makes budgeting much harder for the employee on monthly and quarterly pay cycles, and can also cause stress in not having more frequent income. The familiarity of the bi-weekly schedule helps employees understand the system, allowing them to better budget their cash and is one less hurdle to adapt to when adopting P4P.

Running these numbers for each employee each day is where the actual work comes into play. To begin you'll break the employee's day down by each job they've completed, and gather the subsequent labor revenue totals for each job. To run P4P for that employee, you will total up all of the labor revenue for their entire route, and multiply that by the labor percentage you are paying out. The total P4P generated by that team member is then subject to any applicable manual adjustments. The P4P total for that day can be compared to their base pay, but we will track these separately until the end of the pay period.

Example Time Card: Week 1 of Pay Period

Day	BH for Route	Actual Time to Complete	Calculated P4P (Daily)	Base Pay (Daily)
Mon	8.5	9	182.33	135.00
Tue	8.5	9.25	182.33	138.75
Wed	9	9	193.05	135.00
Thur	8	9	171.60	135.00
Fri	8.5	9.5	182.33	56.25 + 129.38 OT
TOTALS	**42.5**	**45.75**	**911.64**	**729.38**

For the Calculated P4P Daily, let's break down Monday for example:
P4P = (Total Labor Revenue x P4P Percent) +/- Manual Adjustments
P4P = [65 HR * 8.5 BH] x .33)
- 65.00 is the rate we charge the customer per hour.
- 8.5 was the Budgeted Hours for that day's route.
- .33 is the 33% is the Pay for Performance rate we have set to employees.

Example Time Card: Week 2 of Pay Period

Day	BH for Route	Actual Time to Complete	Calculated P4P (Daily)	Base Pay (Daily)
Mon	8.5	6.8	182.33	102.00
Tue	8.5	7.5	182.33	112.50
Wed	9	7.9	193.05	118.50
Thur	8	7.5	171.60	112.50
Fri	8.5	8	182.33	120.00
TOTALS	**42.5**	**37.7**	**911.64**	**565.50**

Fig.4-5

Now when the pay period ends, we have all of the calculations ready to go for Pay Day. We always pay out the higher amount, with all necessary documentation to support the total.

P4P Grand Totals:	Base Pay Grand Totals:
• Week 1 total: 911.64 • Week 2 total: 911.64	• Week 1 total: 600.00 • 129.38 Overtime • Week 2 total: 565.50
$1,823.28 P4P	**$1,294.88 Base Pay**

Once you reach the end of the pay period the sum of both the P4P and base pay are calculated. At this point the higher of the two numbers is paid out to the employee. In accordance with state and federal law, you'll be required to break P4P into its separate components on the employees paystub. This ties back to the importance of tracking their base pay along with the P4P. Their pay stub will show their hourly rate at base pay for their hours clocked in, followed by their overtime pay as recorded. Finally, as a bonus they will receive their remaining performance dollars.

Employee: Zach Phillips	Date: Example week 1 - week 2
Hours: 77.7 Base Pay (15.00/hr): 1,165.50 P4P Bonus: 528.40	Overtime Hours: 5.75 Overtime: 129.38 Manual Adjustments: 0.00 **Total Pay: 1,823.28**

In this example the employee is making the equivalent of $21.85/hr on P4P compared to their $15/hr base pay. Other additions, like quarterly profit sharing, up-sells and referral bonuses will also be added to the bonus section of their paystub.

Fig.6-7

Let's look at an example of a multi day project on the schedule. This same employee with the same variable factors has a project to complete Monday, Tuesday and Wednesday- here's how we'll track it.

* Mezinger Project: 22 Budgeted Hours, Multi day Project

Example Time Card: Week 1 of 2nd Pay Period

Day	BH for Route	Actual Time to Complete	Calculated P4P (Daily)	Base Pay (Daily)
Mon	7.33*	7	105.00 ->	105.00
Tue	7.33*	8	120.00 ->	120.00
Wed	7.33*	5.5	246.90** Mezinger Project Complete	82.50
Thur	8	7.5	171.60	112.50
Fri	8.5	8	182.33	120.00
TOTALS	**38.49**	**36**	**$825.83**	**$540.00**

** Let's break down how we tracked the Mezinger Project:
- The total BH for the project was 22.

- For us that was best split up into 3 days, 7.33 BH for each day (22/3= 7.33).

- At the end of the day when the project was incomplete (Monday and Tuesday) base pay is used as a placeholder in the P4P calculation.

- On Wednesday when the project is completed, then we can calculate the P4P. The total P4P for the Project was $471.90. Because the Base Pay was used as a placeholder for Monday and Tuesday, we subtract these from the total P4P of the project for Wednesday's calculation (otherwise it's essentially double dipping). $471.90 - $105.00 - $120.00 = **$246.90**.

Fig.8

Accurately tracking this data is imperative to running P4P within your business. As considering multi day projects, the nuances of tracking each employee becomes complicated. This is where management software comes into play. For a long time we have used excel to manage and track P4P. Using an excel system works, however the room for human error grows with every input into the equations. In order to use excel, one needs to deeply understand the arithmetic as well as allocate time to manage it. To accurately implement P4P, you need to calculate performance dollars everyday for every employee, and make manual adjustments if necessary for that day. To see a more in depth example on how to do this for a larger team, see Appendix A in the back of the book.

The reason for this diligence is to alleviate the guessing game of remembering yellow slips or upselling bonuses from a few days to a week ago. This human error is what will lead to distrust building in your team, and will ultimately lead to failure. Building an excel document that can receive inputs, run the calculations, then track the totals over a period of time is complicated. That's why to help lawn care and landscape business owners on this journey, the Simplified P4P Tracking System was released at *LandscapeBusinessCourse.com*

Through joining the online course you get access to the P4P software that allows you to plug in the numbers for each employee each day, as well as the customized spreadsheet to track those numbers and see exactly where the money is going each week. Now we have developed the program even further to become a stand alone software for any home service industry where you can track each employee each day and get their reports all in one place. This software is the first of its kind, and has been developed and tested behind the scenes for an extended period of time within our franchise system. This new software cuts out the majority of human error and provides the owner with precise data on their business. *P4Psoftware.com* is where you can find this tool, and where you can take running Pay for Performance to the next level. All the calculations are done for you, project pay is divided correctly between employees, and payroll is a breeze to run.

At the end of the day you don't need fancy software to run your business, but it's akin to having the right tool for the right job. The software is just the next step in streamlining your processes, so that one day you can step away from the business and have operations sustain without you. The software allows you or your office team to run P4P in under one minute per employee per day. That is an incredible investment considering that you will reap a 20-30% efficiency increase (1.5-3 hours per day) from each front line team member. If you made it this far into the book it means you are serious about seeing the incredible effects that P4P on your business. You have got past your initial inhibitions and mental blocks about performance pay. For that reason, I would like to give you a secret key. This secret key is required to gain access to P4Psoftware.com. Without this secret key you cannot become a member. The secret key is actually on the front cover of this book. The account number on the check, if you type it on a phone, spells out AUGUSTA... it also is the 7-digit secret code required to sign up for P4Psoftware.com
SHHHHH.... Keep it quiet =)

PS - once you become a member you will get a secret code of your own to share with other business owners you know so they too can unlock the power of P4P.

PSS - Once you sign up for your free trial at P4Psoftware.com you can book a video call with one of our team. They will help you with implementation and figuring out the numbers for your specific business, concerning base pay and percent of revenue share with the employees.

Chapter 10

Reporting P4P | The Ultimate Report Card!

P4P offers more than a better way to pay. By running the performance numbers on our crew daily, we collect more information on the health and productivity of the business. By breaking down this data into digestible pieces we can better apply ourselves to improve in the future, and pinpoint where to direct our efforts. Using P4Psoftware.com we've devised two such ways of analyzing P4P; the "report card" and "scoreboard."

The Employee Report Card

Report cards are geared towards employees to provide them with their daily earnings, as well as other pertinent information such as the progress of projects, manual adjustments and clocked hours. This generates an overview of their current performance, so they have an accurate metric to set goals, double check calculations and debate adjustments. Beyond the numerical implications, the report card acts as a way for the employees to see the direct impacts of their hard work. Again, the goal is to get the compensation as close to the performance as possible. This is why we want to run P4P and send a performance report the day after that work is completed.

Taking a deeper look at the employee report card,

we can see how this system helps build up team members and builds their sense of purpose. The report card contains information about their clocked hours, project status, current P4P earnings and any manual adjustments. The clocked hours keep them informed on their time invested in the current pay period, while allowing them to calculate their base pay. They will be able to compare the difference that P4P makes on their paycheck EVERY SINGLE DAY. They will see the immediate impacts of pushing themselves or being lazy and see what actions raise or lower their daily pay.

The report card also shows the budgeted hours vs clocked hours on large projects. Tracking a project's completion status is incredibly important information for an employee and employer, as this metric helps set daily goals for the project and to better manage time. This also helps set proper expectations for P4P, and when they will receive the performance dollars payout for that project.

Daily Report Card	Name: Jack Keen Date: 10-09-21
Hours Clocked In: 10.00	Project Name: Johnson House
Base Pay Earned: $120.00	Project Budgeted Hours: 15
P4P Earned: $231.00	Total Project Worked Hours: 1
Manual Adjustments: $0.00	Project Status: Started
Notes:	

Performance pay for the applicable day is one of the most important metrics on the report card. This information is a direct representation of the work invested during this time, and allows them to gauge how much more work they may need to achieve their financial goals. Employees that receive report cards like this can have the ease of mind knowing exactly what to expect at the end of the pay period, and therefore can make adjustments throughout the week to meet their goals. Along the same vein, manual adjustments are also reported on this report card. This informs the employee about the actions of their supervisor

Fig.9

and allows them the opportunity to refute the negative claim or receive recognition for their positive adjustment. This direct feedback loop eliminates confusion on their pay stub, and ensures that the management and team are on the same page about the operations of the business.

Providing these daily report cards to your team takes time away from other duties of management, however the positive implications of this daily reporting are profound. By providing this information to your crew, you keep them informed while keeping yourself better informed. With a click of one button on P4Psoftware.com all these reports are created and emailed to each individual employee and manager on a daily basis.

The Scoreboard System

The real power of this reporting comes in the form of the employer scoreboard. This information can be shared with the crew but it's the most effective in the hands of the owner or manager. The breakdown involves manual adjustments, employee scores, the status of ongoing projects, hours clocked and the hours budgeted overall. The employees are scored to show the exact effect each employee is having on the business in terms of efficiency and profits. The scoreboard is a great tool because it can be shared across the business without actually showing the total amount of income for each employee. It is simply a score of individual efficiency. This scoreboard report can be used to spark some competitive juices in your Team, and have prizes for the top performers.

In the following example we assume 33% of labor revenue is being paid to employees.

Name	Score	$Per/Hr Earned	Total Budgeted Hours	Total Revenue
Jason	4.52	$29.98	43.75	$3365.00
Tim	4.61	$26.02	36.88	$2894.42
John	4.64	$24.15	23.42	$1849.81

For these scoreboard examples, we are using $70/hr Rate to Customer, $12.00/hr for Base Pay, and 33% of labor revenue going to the employee.

	Losing Money	Break Even	Profitable
Score	1-2	2	Above 3

An easy way to explain the scoreboard is by using 1, 2, and 3 as benchmarks. At a 2 or below the employee is losing the company money through waste in labor. This means they are consistently hitting base pay and their actual profitability is much lower than that. At a 2 they are usually breaking even, the employer isn't losing any money however neither party sees a profit. This employee would be hitting base often, but their P4P dollars come out to a similar amount. Lastly, a score of 3 or higher is the goal. This indicates that the employee is reaping the benefits of P4P while the employer is seeing a significant cut in wasted labor revenue. At this score they are consistently making above base pay, and provide lower labor costs because of their generated revenue. Calculating this metric is simple, it's as follows:

Total Labor Revenue / (Clocked Time x Base Pay) = Score Metric

Fig.10-11

The total labor revenue in the equation is the total labor revenue assigned to the particular employee. So for example, if they worked 10 hours at $12.00/hr and completed $500.00 in labor revenue then their equation would be $500/(10 x 12) = 4.16. In this case the employee would be crushing it on P4P, and you would see substantial profits. However, if they worked 10 hours at $12.00/hr and only brought in $200.00 of labor revenue (200/(10 x 12)) they would have only scored a 1.67. At this point the employer would be losing money, and the employee would see little to no returns on P4P, assuming they kept this up for the entire pay period. This score metric is the most precise tool to highlight your highest performers and pinpoint your struggling employees. I get a daily scoreboard from the General Managers of all the locations I own. Within 15 seconds I get a feel of the overall profit from the prior day and can observe trends in low or high performers. This type of report is absolutely imperative for any owner that wants to effectively manage their business remotely or not be present on a daily basis. You cannot become isolated from daily operations and think that everything is running efficiently. You need daily triage of your business showing the most important variables of profitability, and in the home service industry, inefficient labor is the biggest reason companies stay unprofitable.

With the scoreboard method, it's important to pay attention to how the score relates to your base pay, percent of labor for P4P, and the rate to customers as you crunch the numbers. Any more or less and the numbers will be slightly different. For instance, changing the base rate greatly affects this metric. Using the same example as above: The base pay is now $18.00/hr, they made the same $500.00 in Labor Revenue in 10 total hours. Their score would be 2.77, compared to the 4.16 productivity from before when the base pay was $12/hr. This is because raising the base pay would close the gap between the floor of their base wage, and what profits are generated. This highlights why you want to keep your base pay as low as possible, while still being competitive to find new applicants. The larger difference between base pay and P4P means the employee will be more incentivized to stay efficient throughout the remainder of the pay period, and avoid costly yellow slips.

Daily reporting can be time consuming, but building out systems to manage these tasks helps manage the workload. When all is said and done, you and your team will benefit significantly from this new information that previously you didn't have access to. With this new insight, you have the ability to make substantial changes in operations to create long lasting benefits throughout your company. The daily report card allows for employees to manage their time and best apply their efforts and yield maximum results. These systems alleviate stressful guessing at their current status on projects, workload and pay, allowing them to take a clear headed approach to problem solving.

A solutions based management style puts the ball back into the employees court to set goals and weed out inefficiencies in their daily operations. The scoreboard allows the management a window into the daily operations, and keeps them up to date on the status of projects, profitability and the well being of the team. Odds are if a high performer drops suddenly there is more going on behind the scenes, addressing those underlying issues will help ensure their personal well being. If someone consistently has a low score, managers can quickly find the weakest staff and pair them up to learn from the highest performers. This strengthens the business as a whole by creating a tight knit team dynamic where the weak can learn from the strong, mentorship connections are made, and everyone has an opportunity to succeed.

Chapter 11

The Employee's Perspective of P4P

I would like to stop here and make a chapter specifically addressing employees. If you are not the owner/manager of a business and have read this book, I must applaud you for getting this far. This is not an easy read and the math alone can scare some away. It is extremely likely that you are pushing for P4P in your current place of employment, or are just learning to grow your own knowledge. Either way, kudos to you!

From the employee's perspective, P4P is like a cold bottle of water after a long day mowing lawns. It's refreshing to finally see a way to get paid based on how hard you work, a system that cuts the subjective biases away revealing an objective pay structure. This is merely a dream for most laborers in the industry, working tirelessly on a significantly lower wage than their managers seemingly doing nothing. If you're a high performing individual, odds are you're sick of hourly and the lack of opportunity it gives. You are demotivated when working with sub-par coworkers that sap the clock and laze around everyday. This Pay for Performance system was built for those who want to push themselves to achieve their goals without artificial standards holding them back. For many, the proposal to make substantially more money without heavily increasing the personal risk is a no brainer. Let's take a look at exactly what's in it for the employee and why P4P is their key to unlocking potential.

You Have Power

There are many of us who work as hard as we can on work ethic alone. Just by showing up and getting that paycheck we are invested in helping the business grow, and providing quality service to customers. We are used to starting out at the bottom and working our way up slowly through hard work and dedication. Many of us also know the stresses of feeling undervalued and under appreciated. Pay for Performance takes uncontrollable factors out of the equation; like age, race, ethnicity, education; things we may reflect on and use as verification for not being compensated reasonably for our efforts. P4P will alleviate factors that shouldn't be in the workplace at all. This can be the subjective hierarchy between who's been there the longest, or even preferential treatment for who is better friends with the owner. These tensions can build overtime and as people come and go through the business, this balance can be hard to maintain. It can feel like we work to the best of our ability every day, but the compensation, and promotions never pay off as we'd hoped.

P4P eliminates someone else's subjective dictation on your paycheck, placing everyone on an even playing field from day one. Everyone is getting the same labor percent of revenue, everyone has the same base pay, and everyone has the same resources. P4P is giving you the power to make more with your hard work. Whether you have the "head down work hard" mentality or the "work smarter not harder" mindset, this system allows you to instantly reap the benefits rather than waiting for dubious pay raises. If you want to make more money the power is directly in your hands, and for those of us that already share the hustle mindset, this system is too good to be true. The reality is that the more efficient each person is, the more the company makes as a whole, and when the business is profitable it can afford to pay the team more. Throughout the next few pages I included some honest feedback from my employees that have used P4P:

When P4P was first introduced, I was honestly pretty confused, but excited to see how much I would be able to make. My first paycheck, I didn't make much in performance dollars. But I saw how once I was getting more efficient and faster and fine tuning my routes, I was making quite a bit more money. It was super rewarding. It was also really great to have access to the company Audible account. It's packed full of great books to help you improve and learn about business. It's been a really great place to work, and be part of such a great team. – Wyatt

I'm a numbers guy. I would be driving on my route and calculating my P4P for the day in my head. I could see how when we were making better P4P, it was directly related to how well the business was doing. It was easy to set sights on making more, because it was exactly what the business needed to be doing better. – Brad

Eventually there is a ceiling to the amount you can earn as an hourly employee, and the business factors this in for what they can afford to pay you year round. In a seasonal business that is especially difficult. The decision made by an employer on an hourly pay structure does not always account for those who "deserve" it most. Usually the nucleus of employees kept throughout Winter or slower months don't correlate with who is the most efficient. Now there is a way to track that and make decisions based on data!

Seasonal work means that even if the owner can afford to pay a higher percent of revenue to employees on P4P they won't, in fact they shouldn't, simply to ensure that when things are slow and fixed costs exceed the revenue earned they aren't losing money hand over fist. P4P gives a fisheye lens view for the employer, and hands each person the responsibility for generating their own revenue. Over time you'll get more efficient and eliminate wasted labor, improving your pay. Further down the line, this could set you up for other opportunities that come your way like being a trainer and project manager bonuses. Since compensation on P4P is a percentage and not a $/hr rate, this breaks the employer/employee tension by paying more when it's available (busy season) and less when things are tight (slow season).

There's No "I" in Team

This employment opportunity made me realize the person I wanted to be. There were many different paths I was facing, and being surrounded by great people, and being part of such a supportive team is what pushed me to go down a path to be someone better and someone more than I thought I could. - Francisco

One of the biggest fears my crew had when we were making this transition was that the culture would suffer. There was fear of competition, that there wouldn't be friendliness, and that crew mates would throw others under the bus at the opportunity to make more. What the actual outcome of P4P brought, was comradery, strength and dependability. We view a positive attitude as an expectation, not an option- and this definitely played a factor. We help the teammate that is struggling, because their success is success for everyone in more profit. We look out for each other, if there's something that needs to be done better we discuss it and come up with solutions, because we expect the same to be done with us. We are a team that dominates, each player starts on the same line, and each person is in charge with how far they can go. The strength this gives us as a team is paramount to what P4P can do for your financially.

There was a client that wanted a "zen" inspired garden installed in his yard. The client was not as good at giving the specifics of what they were looking for, and was more of the "I'll know if I like it when I see it" type of guy. We had been working on the project for a couple of days, and he had gotten really angry with us multiple times, saying that what we had done was not what he was looking for. Every time he would call on the phone, he'd scream at the office staff. I had finally come to a semblance of a plan with him; I would outline a bit of what we would do, check to see if that was what he was looking for, and then continue from there. When offered to have more people come help me on the project, I

111

said yes without hesitation. The sooner we are able to finish this client's project the better, and we can move on with the schedule.

We were coming up on day five of working on this customer's property with very little progress to show for it. After having the customer come out and change his mind twice on one small garden bed, my coworker Austin came to my aid to intervene. He had said, "Sir, we are happy to finish this project to your liking, but we need you to understand today is the last day we will be here to work on the property. The final result of today will be the final result. Please stay with us out here, so we can make sure our progress is to your liking." To my surprise and great relief, the customer had accepted this graciously. It was like he was a whole new client, was pleasant and let us work to finish the project.

I had asked Austin how he knew to say what he did? He said sometimes people need the comfort of others making the decision for them. Not only am I grateful to have my team back me, I am always learning great things from them too. - Ben

Grow Beyond the Grass

Once a month during our meetings, Mike checks in with each one of us to go over our goals. It could be pay related, and Pay for Performance amount we are looking to hit, or it could be a customer service goal; whatever we see improvement in ourselves. During the next check in, we go over if we met that goal, or if it's something to keep striving for. What really hit home for me is that we were always expected to have some kind of goal, and something to be working towards. It was the kind of environment where they want you to improve as a person for your benefit, and that's really special. - Brad

The pay benefits P4P brings to the table alone make the switch worth it. But the opportunities expanding your personal wealth are miniscule to the other avenues P4P opens up in a business. Where the real value lies is what you learn from being so immersed into the business. Our highest performers take what they've learned to start their own businesses and follow their passions beyond working everyday out in the field. Their financial freedom and intellectual growth is a direct result of their hard work, and avenues open up for them to live the sort of life and pursue the dreams they've always wanted to. Looking beyond the daily grind you garner the freedom to allocate your time to pursue your own passions. Once you have taken control of your personal income you are free to be the architect of your own life, building out time to pursue your own passions and having the resources to fund those endeavors. With the knowledge you gained you can pursue avenues of passive income, generating an infrastructure of wealth that can finally alleviate the need to work in the first place. On P4P, these goals go from whimsical fantasy for the few of us privileged enough to make it to the top, to achievable for every individual who puts in the work. Performance pay unlocks the potential for anyone to achieve their dreams no matter their initial skill base or status.

Something that we do here that I've never done at my past landscaping jobs is the Yellow Slip System in P4P. We have to talk to the customer and make right whatever they didn't like or they left a bad review about. We take initiative and we share our mistakes to help everyone learn. This has really helped me personally, as far as public speaking and conquering my fear of it goes. - Ben

As time goes on and we settle into the rhythm of our day we slowly become masters of our craft; cutting out the minor inefficiencies, and swiftly navigating through the problems that arise on a day to day basis. Although life isn't perfect we become increasingly better at navigating it's challenges. This is the goal with P4P: to reach a point where you are constantly making above base pay as a result of the work you've done in the past to improve overall workflow. For leaders on our team, this is already a reality, they no longer pour over their report cards trying to brainstorm new ways to cut out waste. For many this is where they stop, content to make consistently more money out in the field working doing what they do best. However, some of us look at this and wonder "Is that it?", is that the plateau of progress, making some more this month and a little less the next, casually riding the waves of our hard work?

The answer is no, and for many this is just the start. By the time you find yourself coasting well above base pay, odds are that you have already collected on the subsequent bonuses of upselling, project management, and training; this shows that you have already gained the skills to effectively run different aspects of a business. You have already acquainted yourself with the efficiency and cultural pitfalls of your industry and overcome many obstacles new owners face. This points you in the direction of starting your own venture, just another step of taking on more risk to greater your reward. Beyond starting your own business, however, there is even more opportunity that awaits those who conquer the day to day grind. Building upon your experience gained under the system of "Open Book Management" and working within the Pay for Performance system, you will inevitably gain skills that can propel you forward into other career paths. Skills like project management, customer service, and team leadership (just to name a few) are incredibly desired and marketable skills. Your experience can be applied in different avenues to sustain your longevity in the workforce and your upward mobility in life.

When I first met my then girlfriend's parents, she had recalled me describing my profession to them as, "I'm like a landscaper, lawn care guy. I can do patios sometimes, and make yards look really nice." She had recalled my timidness, and embarrassment toward the subject, as if I was worried they'd judge me.

Fast forward to today, I wear Augusta proud on my chest. I am more than happy to tell anyone willing to listen about my experiences here, and to share the powerful message Augusta is here to give. It's not just show up, make a decent mow route, and try to make sure everyone gets off at the same time. I show up here to help change the professionalism in the industry, to help create systems and business practices that will make everyone better and thriving. I'm here, and part of this team; someone who had no experience, and was able to grow by working hard and showing up. - Lee Park

The Conversation of P4P

More often than you'd expect, motivated employees are in the position where they want to pitch the P4P system to the owner, making differences from the bottom up. Although this can be a tricky situation, we have seen this happen within our own organization. The employees that have the best success in this endeavor place themselves in the position of a salesman. By removing personal biases and considering the wants and needs of their employer, a more constructive conversation can take place. If you are an employee and want to convince your employer that P4P is the way of the future; make sure you focus on THEIR pain points, how P4P solves THEIR problems, and how P4P makes THEM more money! P4P offers two main advantages to an employer, firstly the system eliminates wasted labor on inefficient employees. Secondly, it affords the ability to pay the team more without affecting their overall profits. Owners find themselves in the position where employees are constantly asking for raises, based on arbitrary metrics like how long they've worked there instead of based on work ethic. If employers can afford to pay employees more they typically do, however most aren't profitable enough to afford these extra expenditures. What other pain points could P4P solve for your employer? You have learned these throughout this book. If they complain about lazy employees being on their phones, damage to company property, unhappy clients calling, or people not showing up to work, those are the points you want to emphasize.

Highlighting pain points that you can see from your position will typically highlight underlying issues from their perspective. Preeminent to achieve any form of success when educating your employer, you'll want to ensure you are coming from a position of offering solutions to help the business, rather than pushing your own incentives on them. Simply pointing them in the direction of resources like this book or videos online can be enough for them to come to their own conclusions on the system. You might not be credited with changing the business for the better, but through your actions you have made a difference in your future, the future of the business, and the well being of your coworkers. If change for your coworkers and your owner is truly your goal, you won't concern yourself with being recognized as the "savior" that initiated the change. Let your owner come to the same conclusion about P4P that you have, and think they did it on their own.

In the case of high performers or veteran team members, P4P might entail lowering their base pay. If you are already substantially above base pay on your current hourly structure, it can be hard to consider making the shift. In theory you could make more but there is no guarantee, it can feel like a step backwards. This can be the hardest part of rolling out this new system, however P4P gives the employer the ability to pay their highest performers more. The employer can't guarantee that they'll have enough work to justify paying someone substantially more, thus capping the employees earnings lower than they can afford on occasion. This means that even if the owner can afford to pay more they won't simply from the fear of the financial pressure that was created the last time they doled out a raise/bonus. Pay for Performance breaks this tension by paying more when it's available and less when things are tight. However in this case when the business pays less its not to save the profits for the owner its because other inefficiencies are pulling at the company's resources. This places us in the position to brainstorm solutions to address the stressors rather than a reactionary position where we are just trying to stay afloat. By taking on more risk with P4P you allow yourself the opportunity to reap a larger reward. Tying the business closer to each employee allows each individual to make a more meaningful impact on their personal success, but also the collective success of the business.

My biggest advice to make these big changes, is to just do it. These big decisions can be paralyzing, a fear of the unknown. But you don't need to wait until tomorrow to make the right decision when you can make the right decision today. Once you've taken the first step, the rest fall into place.
- Brad

Chapter 12

P4P 2.0 | Profit Sharing

Open Book Management holds us accountable to create a fair and subjective form of profit sharing, so that the team could understand the numbers behind their bonus and trust in our system. This led us into building clear guidelines on how to receive profit sharing and what exactly that was. As you might expect, it was much easier to introduce profit sharing than P4P, but it was still important to us to have a sturdy framework around our system.

Once we've successfully opened the teams eyes to cutting waste from their labor, now all eyes are on the profit. Eventually the individualism of P4P will push focus on their personal profit over that of the business, but by offering profit sharing you curb that narrative, as the single action of one dictates the team's earnings as a whole. Now if the company gets equipment stolen then they stole from "US", and if equipment is broken then "OUR" equipment is damaged. They begin to care, because those costs come out of their profits at the end of the quarter. Team meetings and inspirational speeches will only go so far to garner the attention of the team, you need to affect their pockets. Bottom line: they won't care about the numbers in open book management unless it moves the needle for their paycheck.

Once P4P is in place and profit margins increase

dramatically, you want to ensure that this remains the constant focus. To do this, you must give your employee a piece of the pie. This is extremely important if you are not at the business on a daily basis and have very high profit margins. It is hard to motivate the Team to increase profits if they feel that money is just lining your personal pockets. Give them a piece of the action and they will stay hungry for more.

Incentives

Profit Sharing much like P4P was born out of frustration, and determination to elevate my team to a higher standard. When we first implemented the Pay for Performance system, it had a tendency of bringing out the best and worst qualities in people. In this case, it was a team member who could roll up late, while their coworker got everything ready for the day; but would be paid the same because they ran the route together and split the labor revenue commissions they earned for that day. As a painfully punctual individual this burned at my core, I could see how much it annoyed my team as much as myself.

In my eyes, there were two ways of addressing the issue; policy or incentives. Policy-driven organizations have strict rules around being late and calling out without notice. The problem I faced was when times are tough and we have packed schedules, I knew I wouldn't be able to follow through and fire people. Incentives on the other hand have a similar side approach to P4P, incentivise the desirable behavior using profit sharing. Stop pushing, bribing, reprimanding them for unwanted behavior and focus on highlighting, incentivizing, and applauding the opposite actions. For an employee to receive a portion of profit sharing, they must meet the requirements laid out for them on the P4P document (Appendix A) during the onboarding process. This allowed us to build the culture to fit our needs while helping the team. There is no decision to be made whether a team member should receive the profit sharing or not. They either met the requirements or didn't, potentially losing out on a bonus that quarter.

What requirements you hold your team accountable for depends on what you need from your team, and the areas you want to incentivize. That's the nice part. Unlike P4P, where numbers and formulas reign supreme, profit sharing has an element of subjectivity based on which behaviors you want to promote and incentive. If something annoys you constantly, make that the metric by which profit sharing is determined. Our criteria for profit sharing includes the team member to be present for the entire quarter without any unexcused absences, and without showing up late to their shifts. This doesn't mean that they can't call out sick, but rather they need to contact us as soon as possible. In our case, that's at least two hours before their shift starts. Odds are, if an employee is sick they'll know a couple hours before work starts, and we want them to give us as much heads up around that as possible. Similarly, if an employee wants days off or to use their PTO (Paid Time Off), we need to know in advance so that we can schedule around their absence. With our traditionally lean crews in the labor market, it's as important as ever to have good communication around scheduling, and profit sharing helps manage that.

When it comes to being late as the first offense, the team member loses half of their quarterly profit sharing. After the second tardy, they lose the rest. We only hold half on the first offense to give them room to correct their behavior, rather than cracking down and demotivating them the remainder of the quarter. While this system doesn't work for everyone, it helps us show appreciation to those who ensure operations are running smoothly by being on time. Of course negative behavior like consistent tardiness and call-outs with short notice need more drastic attention, typically that involves firing that individual. However in most cases we have seen that this profit sharing helps incentivise the team to be on time, and give us a heads up if they are needing time off.

How does Profit Sharing look for you?

When determining exactly what this percentage is, it's up to you. My method is to base the percent of profits shared off how profitable the business is, as well as how involved I am. Because this is based on percentage, it means you can still implement this when you are running a crew of one or two employees. If you made $30,000 in profits in a specific quarter and have two employees eligible for a 10% profit share, that would mean that each of them could make $1500 assuming they didn't get any deductions.

What if you are unprofitable? I would still institute a profit sharing program so that employees know that once profitability is achieved there is a benefit to them personally. One of our Augusta franchisees joined with an existing independent lawn care business. They had over $100,000 in debt and asked if they should start profit sharing. I told them to put a large thermometer in their shop that reflected the amount of debt they still owed. They told the Team that when all the debt was paid off the profit sharing program would begin. What gets measured, gets managed. Sure enough in the 1.5 years of being with Augusta and starting P4P, they paid all the debt off and started sharing profits with the Team.

But I digress... everyone wants to know what percent of profits to share with employees. I look at it in two groups which are managers and the front line crew. A good starting point is 5%, and working your way up from there as your business grows. It's important to remember that growth sucks cash, so if you are in the stage of growing your business there might not be many profits to speak of. However as your business matures, your profits begin to become more accessible, and that's when you can start leveraging them as a tool to incentivize your team.

For example, at the time of this writing, I own Augusta locations in Washington, North Carolina, and Connecticut. I never spend time at the NC and CT locations. I trust my General Manager to keep the place running and make all hiring, buying, and marketing decisions. That's why I give those General Managers 25% of profits every quarter. 10% of profits are shared with front line team members as well. Since I'm not there ensuring the quality and productivity of my staff, I need the GMs to think more like owners and guard the bottom line of which a large chunk of their annual compensation consists. On the flip side, at the original Augusta location, I spend time there every week with the team, perhaps 30-40 minutes per week. Because of my direct involvement, I only do 10-5% profit sharing for managers at that location. In addition to the managers profit sharing, the front line staff also split 10% of profits evenly each quarter. Again, this is ONLY IF they are eligible and have not lost their right to the profit sharing by being late or absent. If they have lost their profit sharing privileges, that money does not go back into the profit sharing pool. It is kept in the business to cover the cost to the company when schedules have to be rearranged to tardies and unexcused absences. If you are at the stage where your business is running without you, profit sharing can be your way of ensuring quality and innovation. This frees you of responsibilities, and you can invest your time in other areas.

When we talk about profits and using incentives to drive engagement in the workplace, one of the most common examples is a "damage pool". If you are unfamiliar, it typically means the owner puts up a dollar amount in the beginning of the time frame. This can be by month, quarter or year, and every damage case, tardy, and absence is taken out of that pool of money. For example, if they put up $5,000.00 in the pool for the quarter and Tim was late, that's -$100.00. Then a window broke. That's around -$250.00 and so on, until the end of the period where the remaining money is divided amongst the team. I'm not a fan of this method, especially over profit sharing for a few reasons.

The first reason damage pools don't work is they hold arbitrary amounts that have no real weight in the business. The team has no impact on this amount beyond their negative impacts. With P4P and open book management, our goal is to teach the team about the business and give them the information and tools to work better throughout their day while improving themselves overall. By sharing profits they feel the direct impact of how the business is doing, and how their actions affect it. If you want them to think like owners you have to pay them like owners.

When we give the ability to our team to think like owners, we aren't giving them full "owner" decision making rights. However, when they get a piece of profits suddenly your team cares much more when you are buying new equipment, trucks and so on. Here's why; because that expense is coming directly out of how much they will make at the end of that quarter. You might find yourself defending your actions and coming into clashes with the crew about how that profit is allocated in the business. As terrifying and frustrating this can be as an owner, it is much better than the alternative. I would rather them be engaged and disagree with the decision than be passively content with whatever the profits of the business are. If your team is engaged to this extent, then they may be able to offer insights and advice that you might have overlooked. The employees on the front lines, closest to the work itself, usually have the best ideas and first hand experience of waste in the workplace. They will care far more about the equipment and trucks because they feel involved in their acquisition. This doesn't mean bending to the whim of your employees, but it does hold you accountable to justify your decisions, and gives you the opportunity to educate your team on why these are the right decisions. I would have never thought that I would be explaining amortization, expense depreciation or tax implications to a group of landscape employees... but they actually care and now understand valuable financial concepts.

Though tension can arise in this new circumstance, you will find that your team will be more keenly invested in the success of the business. The more we can get the team working toward the success of the business, the more likely we will succeed.

Chapter 13

The P4P Ecosystem and Personal Elevation

P4P caused a radical shift throughout every facet of our company. From the people to the operations, and through it all our business has been strengthened, and our crew is flourishing. Building this system brick by brick allows us to see what potential Pay for Performance really has. By initially gathering your numbers, you can be assured that this shift won't have catastrophic implications, and you begin to see the possibilities it offers. Take the next step and build a framework to support P4P, by introducing policies like the yellow slips and team meetings. You have now successfully prepared yourself to start your strategic deployment. Bring your team on board through the initial trial period. They'll become more engaged in the company overall, and set the wheels in motion. With the bolstered support of your team, your company begins to make the shift towards a brighter future.

This new alignment within your company shuts down the draining tug of war sustained by the futile hourly pay structure, and contrives a battering ram of progress. Bashing down the walls holding you back from growing your business, you become part of a team rather than the opponent. The aim of you and your compatriots lock on to the true target of running a business; profit. Once the true goal is revealed and all parties have the proper incentives to pursue it, then progress comes naturally. Pay for Performance is the vehicle that propels you towards your goals, but ultimately you are the driver.

Taking the helm of this ship is no simple task. The calculation commitment far exceeds that of hourly and the accumulation of data must be properly managed or the ship will go down. A skilled captain navigates these challenges given the right tools and experience to do so. By using P4Psoftware.com we can consume the information and recite useful data. The daily report card and scoreboard are examples of the powerful tools now in the hands of you and your team. Through combining our knowledge of the industry with a new perspective of our business, we can sail the stormy waters to fertile fishing grounds well beyond our shores.

But what does this success look like? After years in the industry you begin to ask yourself if this is enough, if you are reaching your goals. As the seasons come and go, I got to the point where I began looking beyond myself, and started reflecting on helping others. This narrative runs through my entire life: from doing charity work early on with my church, to eventually studying to become a doctor. Helping others is in my blood and nothing changed when I became a business owner. I franchised Augusta Lawn Care to help those in the industry who couldn't manage all responsibilities of a business on their own or tried and had failed. This fostered the idea of helping the industry as a whole by being that rising tide, to raise the level of professionalism. To annihilate the idea of the poor dirty landscaper with little to offer. Landscaping isn't a career to be scoffed at, it's a true profession. I hope that one day it is looked at as a respectable trade. This will come about by using many systems, new technologies, and innovations, of which P4P is one. As we grew, I looked at those around me and stuck out a hand to lift them up. We built the 3F (Franchise Fee Forgiveness) program, to give other owners a chance to make their goals a reality. Through all of this I found success, but it wasn't until we started fostering the success of others that I truly felt like I had achieved something. The story of an individual who paved the path for others to follow is truly one worth telling and a life worth living.

Nic Reed will Succeed

Nic Reed faced many challenges growing up that impacted the kind of person he is today. Factors like tight budgets, moving multiple times between divorced parents, and trying to make it through okay was difficult. At times he had to take a two hour bus ride to school and back. He wasn't able to relate to his peers because of how different his situation was, and he felt that divide.

In April of 2019, he started working at Augusta. At the time he was living with roommates he didn't get along with. Augusta, when he applied, was a means to an end. This changed when he was welcomed into a team, where we look out for each other, and always extend a hand to lift those struggling. It was eye opening, an opportunity to be something more than the dead end path he was on. As he reflected on his new reality, he knew a major shift needed to happen in order for this positive change to have a chance at truly changing his life.

P4P started hitting his paychecks week after week. Suddenly he was there early setting up for the day and talking numbers at our optional "Midweek Motivation Meetings." He was learning, taking initiative and most importantly, he was determined. The gears were turning in his head and when the opportunity arose to swap his car for a van he jumped on the chance. He knew in order to open as many doors as possible for himself, that funding was the key factor. So he made the decision to move into that van in August of 2019 for one whole year. He would save up all the money from his paychecks, and see how far that could get him.

It was a rocky transition; showers had to be strategic, food was pretty low quality, and the fall/winter nights were cold and wet. He had to be careful where he parked. Sometimes certain parking lots didn't feel the safest with just a pane of glass separating him from everyone else.

There was a point where a burnt pot of black beans meant for dinner had ingrained a foul smell in the van, and all the windows and doors were left open during daylight to try and eliminate it.

It was that destined winter during a snowstorm a semblance of a path was formed. It was January, and we were rolling into hour 18 of nonstop plowing. Sitting in the truck with Brad, one of his coworkers, it turned into a conversation of "what if?" What if he could open his own Augusta location? What would he have to do to make that happen? How would this happen? This thought persisted in the back of his mind the following weeks.

He started self evaluating. He would ask in-depth questions about his P4P, and his profit sharing; things like, "If I help this person over here with mulch and then drop off this shovel to the other person, where is my P4P coming from and does that affect theirs?" or, "If I'm trying to get this project done and I leave for lunch but get gas as I eat, do I need to clock out?" It had gotten to the point of questioning when my office manager set up a time for him to meet and go over numbers weekly with Loni, the office assistant at the time. To us, he was really taking initiative to succeed with the system.

Time went by and Nic had moved up to the big leagues. He was managing projects and upselling jobs on the fly. He had gone from a troubled kid to our model employee and that's when he finally came to me with the big idea. He wanted to start his own location and I was determined to help him reach that goal. Together we laid the groundwork for the 3F (Franchise Fee Forgiveness) program and Nic was to be our first recipient. After working within the company, understanding our systems and processes, he was miles ahead of the curb, and deeply in tune with the culture we try to foster.

When he had first told his girlfriend and mom about what he was going to do, they were very apprehensive. Many questions were asked and when a business hasn't started yet, there's not always answers. We were confident in Nic's success, because not only did he prove himself as an employee, he had proven himself with his character. He was determined, empathetic, and hardworking. He put in the work to ensure he could train properly and sufficiently to get a new employee up to standards. He made sure he had the leadership within him to run his own team. He learned everything about P4P so he could run the numbers and trust that he could be a reliable employer.

He got set up with his own territory in Marysville, WA and within months was seeing staggering growth. The first year in business he did over $200,000 in revenue, with just one employee, and purchased a third truck to continue his growth. I covered the initial fees so he could reinvest the money he had saved from living in the van to launching his Augusta location with a bang! Nick was the first, but because of him, many would have the opportunity to follow in his footsteps.

Be the Change You Wish to See in the World

None of this would have been possible if it weren't for the integration of P4P as a whole. Many people see its individual parts like profit sharing and open book management as separate and optional. However, just like anything else, we need these systems to facilitate the overall flow. With only fragments of the puzzle, we can never complete the image. P4P relies on profit sharing to unite the team by shining a spotlight on the product of our labor. Employees are as much a part of making daily operations run smoothly as they are about protecting the bottom line. Giving them bonuses has less effect on culture, however if they are detached from the numbers they are prompted to care about. If they are supposed to care about the business they need to be equipped with information and data; that is the objective of open book management.

These systems work in symbiosis, supporting each other and strengthening the company as a whole. Thanks to their intentional integration they work to foster the growth of individuals within your team, and promote a culture of innovation. Create an environment where you can cultivate talent instead of managing a revolving door of faces. Those who come and go from your company are equipped with the tools to make a better life for themselves and pursue their ambitions. As shown in the graphic, there is a 3-layered pyramid to build a great team culture that is also extremely profitable. P4P is the base foundation of the pyramid that open book management is built on. Profit sharing is built on top of open book management and is the capstone of a solid company culture where everyone defends the bottom line. This 3-layered system must be built in this sequence from bottom to top. This organizational structure and the cultural and economical benefits garnered is an order of magnitude more effective when all three are combined together. P4P isn't the answer to all the problems a business faces in its lifetime but it is designed to address one of the most pressing issues of our current labor market.

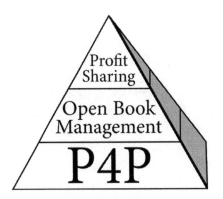

Labor jobs are typically viewed as the bottom of the barrel, work that no one wants to do, but somebody's gotta do it. Job security and potential riches lie in doing the work no one else wants to do. P4P questions that narrative by suggesting that it can be far more than a means to an end. By fostering a collaborative culture where people come to learn and grow together, the work becomes secondary to the benefits that you gain in your daily experience. Work becomes meaningful and full of purpose by becoming an intriguing problem to solve each day, the problem of maximizing time to achieve your goals. If this doesn't sound like work that's because the current problem is the exact opposite. It's to expend as much time as possible to prolong

Fig.12

the completion of each task. Flipping the narrative, work becomes a place where we learn and grow and have lasting effects on our careers and lives as a whole.

Work in the labor field is unique as the bar to entry is incredibly low. Literally any person can pick up the skills of the trade simply by applying enough time to learn them. This should set up labor to be akin to that of an apprenticeship or internship, but this is far from the case. The full picture of Pay for Performance challenges that. Why can't this industry be a place for young entrepreneurs to get started, and learn the core values of business while filling a void in our workforce? I can speak from experience that you learn far more from working in a business with open book management and profit sharing than you do getting your business degree. The sheet of paper a degree affords however, costs much more and has little impact on actually guaranteeing your success in the future labor economy.

As we move into the future and our work becomes increasingly automated, we will start to see the disappearance of simple repetitive tasks. This is the cross hairs resting on the labor industry and when the tech industry lands their shot we will need a competitive edge to stay relevant. Our ability to adapt and provide that human element is exactly that edge. We can act as a stepping stone to foster the talent of the future while providing our customers with unmatched human connection. Even if we end up being the ones piloting the automatons of the future, our core values will still be applicable and will become our true value proposition.

P4P stands for Pay for Performance. It's as simple as that. Your team should be paid for the service they are providing to you, just as much as the customer is paying you for the service you are providing them. The simplicity is key and that is why P4P works. Once you open up the books and show the team the impact they have, the system takes care of the rest. This isn't a band aid solution, it is addressing the root cause of the issue. The battle between employees and employers needs to come to an end. If you are tired of fighting, then P4P is the answer.

Sample P4P Policy: Augusta Lawn Care

Appendix A

Pay-For-Performance (P4P) System

The objective of implementing P4P is to allow for high-performers to be paid more. Low performers might make less and may leave. This creates a meritocracy by which the more efficient a Team member is, the more they will be compensated. This aligns the goals of the company and employee around high quality, reduction of yellow slips, and improved efficiency while removing a pay ceiling for experienced Team members.

The P4P System will be revised and added to on a continual basis to improve efficiency and fairness.

Mowing/Maintenance Routes
1.) 33% of labor revenue paid to the Team
)From March - May 40% of labor revenue)
2.) Pay period compensation cannot average less than $18/hour
3.) If a Team member is training a new employee, $4 per hour will be added to their day, as decided by OWNER/MANAGER.

Landscaping/Cleanups/Large First Time Mows
1.) 33% of labor revenue paid to the Team
2.) Pay period check cannot average less than $18/hour...
3.) Jobs at/over 49 budgeted hours will have $1.50 per budgeted hour bonus. This will be 100% subject to how the OWNER/MANAGER wants to divide the bonus. This will be based upon who managed the job, loaded materials early, communicated with the client and office.
4.) If a multi-day job runs over a pay period end-date, hours will be paid out at base pay. After a project is complete, performance dollars are allocated.

Other Policies:

1.) **Maintenance Time or Paid Non-Billable Hours** require approval from the office manager. (Paid at base rate of $18/hr).

2.) **$50 Cash Bonus** for NEW Customer Referral that accepts any landscape or mowing estimate. Name, Address, Email and Phone Number Required of the potential client. $10 Gift Cards will be given if an EXISTING Customer accepts an estimate that was initiated by a Team member.

3.) **Yellow Slips:** "Guilty" Team member(s) must return to fix the job. If an alternate Team member has to fix the job, they will be paid by-the-hour and that will be deducted from the "guilty" Team member. Yellow Slips will be recorded on Employee Profiles.

4.) **Damaged Property:** Damage case will be recorded on the Employee's Profile. Costs of damages can be removed from the performance dollars (anything over $18/hr) on a given pay period. The base pay will still be honored and money cannot be withdrawn from multiple pay periods. This will incentivize caution and care around customer and company property/equipment.

5.) **Quality Control for Weeding or Mowing:** If weeding/mowing service is skimped on the office can take away the pay from the Team member that performed service in prior visits and give it to the person that has to spend more time to get the property to an appropriate standard.

6.) **Tools and Equipment:** You want to set up the crew after you for success. Failing to organize tools or properly end the day on your truck/equipment may result in a deduction if the crew after you has to pick up your slack. These decisions will be resolved and decided by the office manager.

7.) **Grey Areas:** Any debate between Team members or how much commission should go to who will be settled by OWNER/MANAGER, and their decision and allocation of funds will be final.

Other Information:

Profit Sharing Program:
10% of quarterly profits shared to full time in-field Team Members
Quarters: March - May, June - August, September - November, December - February

1.) Team member(s) must work the entire quarter from start to finish to participate.
2.) Unexcused absence or being late one day will HALF your profit sharing. The second late arrival or absence will result in no quarterly profit sharing

Weekly Scoreboard:
Shows weekly progress on landscape jobs and a team average for the mowing crew.
If the mowing average is 2.0: we break even. 3.0+ is the goal.

Compiled P4P Equations
Appendix B

Equation Key	
Outcome	**Equation**
P4P Solo Mow	P4P = Budgeted Hours x Hourly Rate Charged x % Labor Revenue **P4P = BH x HRC x LR%**
P4P Team Mow	P4P = (Budgeted Hours x Hourly Rate Charged x % Labor Revenue) / # of People **P4P = (BH x HRC x LR%) / # P** *# replaceable variable*
Base Pay	Base Pay = Base Hourly Rate x Hours Clocked + Overtime Rate x Overtime Hours **BP = (BHR x HC) + (OT x OTH)**
Project Manager Bonus	Project Manager Bonus = Project Manager Bonus Rate * Budgeted Hours **PMB = PMBR x BH**
Project P4P	P4P = (Personal Clocked Time) / 31.1 (Total Clocked Time) x 32 (Budgeted Hours) x $70 Hourly Rate Charged) x .33 (% Labor Revenue)) - (Base Pay Place Holders) **P4P = (PCT / TCT x BH x HRC x LR%) - (PH)**
Training Bonus	Training Bonus = Clocked Time (training) x Training Bonus Rate **TB = CT(training) x $?/Hr**

Example P4P Calculations
Appendix C

For this section, please refer to the following "Key" as well as the "Abbreviation Key". We will be going through an actual P4P Pay Period that occurred in 2021. We will see training bonuses, multi day projects, and a damage case. Once you feel comfortable how the calculations come together as we look at Thomas, Dale and Joseph's P4P, try doing Andy's yourself to make sure you're grasping the concept.

Key	
Labor Revenue %	33%
Base Rate	$15.00
Time Off	
Hourly Rate to Customer	$70.00

Abbreviation Key	
Labor Revenue %	LR%
Base Pay	BP
Placeholder	PH
Hours	Hr
3 People	3 P
2 People	2 P
Overtime	OT
Adjustments	+ / -
Training Bonus	TB
Clocked Time	CT
Personal Clocked Time	PCT
Total Clocked Time	TCT
Budgeted Hours	BH
Hourly Rate to Customer	HRC
Week 1	Wk 1
Week 2	Wk 2

Sample Week 1

EMP.	Joseph	Andy	Dale	Thomas
Sat/ Sun	$50.79 *Training Bonus (+$4/hr, 3.4 Hr) (3.22 BH 2 P Mow)		$37.19 (3.22 BH 2 P Mow)	
Mon	$165.97 *Training Bonus (+$4/hr, 9.9 Hr) (9.44 BH 2 P Mow) (.75 BH Solo Mow)	? (8 BH Solo)	$109.03 (9.44 BH 2 P Mow)	
Tue	$185.38 *Training Bonus (+$4/hr, 9.5 Hr) (9.26 BH 2 P Mow) (1.75 BH Solo Mow)	? (8 BH Solo)	$106.95 (9.26 BH 2 P Mow)	
Wed	$154.58 *Training Bonus (+$4/hr, 9.8 Hr) (8.99 BH 2 P Mow) (.5 BH Solo Mow)	? (13.39 BH Solo)	$103.83 (8.99 BH 2 P Mow)	
Thur	$124.80 *Training Bonus (+$4/hr, 8.9 Hr) (3.59 BH 3 P Mow) (3.33 BH 2 P Mow) (1 BH Solo Mow)	? (3.59 BH 3 P Mow) (3.13 BH Solo Mow)	$66.10 (3.59 BH 3 P Mow) (3.33 BH 2 P Mow)	
Fri	$184.96 *Training Bonus (+$4/hr, 9.8 Hr) (7.46 BH 2 P Mow) (2.58 BH Solo Mow)	? *Training Bonus (+$4/hr, 8 Hr) *Lander Project (9.36 CT)	$86.16 (7.46 BH 2 P Mow)	$216.10 *Lander Project (9.36 CT)

Sample Week 2

EMP.	Joseph	Andy	Dale	Thomas
Sat/ Sun				
Mon	$169.30 *Training Bonus (+$4/hr, 9.7 Hr) *Morrison Project (8.7 CT)	? *Training Bonus (+$4/hr, 8.8 Hr) *Damage Case: -$125.00 (10.44 BH 2 P Mow)	$87.00 *Morrison Project (5.8 CT)	$120.58 (10.44 BH 2 P Mow)
Tue	$169.30 *Training Bonus (+$4/hr, 9.7 Hr) *Morrison Project (8.7 CT)	? *Training Bonus (+$4/hr, 9.4 Hr) (10.78 BH 2 P Mow)	$96.00 *Morrison Project (6.4 CT)	$124.51 (10.78 BH 2 P Mow)
Wed	$294.60 *Training Bonus (+$4/hr, 9.5 Hr) *Morrison Project COMPLETE (8.7 CT) (5.92 BH 2 P Mow)	? *Training Bonus (+$4/hr, 8.6 Hr) (10.41 BH 2 P Mow)	$175.35 (5.92 BH 2 P Mow) (Morrison Project Complete)	$120.24 (10.41 BH 2 P Mow)
Thur	$157.90 *Training Bonus (+$4/hr, 9.1 Hr) *Burgess Project (8.1 CT)	? (9.37 BH Solo Mow)	$76.50 *Burgess Project (5.1 CT)	
Fri	$259.06 *Training Bonus (+$4/hr, 8.9 Hr) *Burgess Project COMPLETE (8 CT)	? *Burgess Project COMPLETE (8 CT)	$146.33 *Burgess Project COMPLETE (5.3 CT)	

The Projects have an additional spot for tracking, to ensure everyone who works them gets the proper amount of P4P. Here's the projects from this pay period:

Morrison Project, 32 BH	Running Clocked Hours	PCT
Joseph	8.7+8.7+1.5	18.9
Dale	5.8+6.4	12.2
TOTAL		31.1 TCT

Burgess Project, 32 BH	Running Clocked Hours	PCT
Joseph	8.1+8	16.1
Dale	5.1+5.3	10.4
Andy	8	8
TOTAL		34.5 TCT

Lander Project, 18.71 BH	Running Clocked Hours	PCT
Andy	9.355	9.355
Thomas	9.355	9.355
TOTAL		18.71 TCT

Calculating the P4P:

<u>Let's start with Thomas, Week 1:</u>

He only worked one day, on the Lander Project with Andy.

For Thomas' portion; we will take his personal clocked time divided by total clocked time, multiplied by the budgeted hours, hourly rate charged, % labor revenue; and subtract any Base Pay placeholder amounts from previous days.

Fri = (9.355 (personal clocked time) / 18.71 (Total clocked time) x 18.71 (Budgeted Hours) x $70 (hourly rate charged) x .33 (% labor revenue)) - $0.00 (he only worked on the project one day, no placeholders were used)

Fri = (9.355 PCT / 18.71 TCT x 18.71 BH x $70 HRC x .33 LR%) - $0.00 PH

Crunch the numbers, you should get $216.10 P4P, Week 1 for Thomas.

<u>Thomas' Week 2 Calculations:</u>

He was being trained by Andy on a mowing route during his three days of working. We will take the budgeted hours (you'll see this on the schedule) Multiplied by the hourly rate charged, the labor revenue percent; this sum divided by 2 for 2 people on the route. Note that this will be done for each day, and we'll compile the totals for the weekly total.

Mon = (10.44 BH x $70 HRC x .33 LR%) / 2 P
Mon = $120.58 P4P

Tue = (10.78 BH x $70 HRC x .33 LR%) / 2 P
Tue = $124.51 P4P

Wed = (10.41 BH x $70 HRC x .33 LR%) / 2 P
Wed = $120.24 P4P

We'll add these up, and the total P4P Week 2 for Thomas: $365.33.

While the P4P is calculated, we know for Week 1 his total hours was 7.92; multiplied by his base pay equals $118.80. Week 2 his total hours were 24.22; multiplied by base pay is $363.30; bringing the sum of weeks 1 & 2 to $482.10

Next, we will calculate for Dale, Week 1:

Dale was also being trained on a mowing route, by Joseph.

Sat/Sun = (3.22 BH x $70 HRC x .33 LR%) / 2 P
Sat/Sun = $37.19 P4P

Mon = (9.44 BH x $70 HRC x . 33 LR%) / 2 P
Mon = $109.03 P4P

Tue = (9.26 BH x $70 HRC x . 33 LR%) / 2 P
Tue = $106.95 P4P

Wed = (8.99 BH x $70 HRC x . 33 LR%) / 2 P
Wed = $103.83 P4P

Thursday has an extra factor, part of the day was a 2 person mow route, and part of the day was a 3 person mow route. Here's the breakdown:

Thur = ((3.59 BH x $70 HRC x .33 LR%) / 3 P) + ((3.33 BH x $70 HRC x .33 LR%) / 2 P)
Thur = $27.64 + $38.46
Thur = $66.10 P4P

It's the exact same equation being added together, one with the 3 person factor and the second with the 2 person factor, calculated separately and then added together.

Fri = (7.46 BH x $70 HRC x .33 LR%) / 2 P
Fri = $86.16 P4P

Add the totals for Wk 1, Total P4P for Dale is $509.26.

Dale's Calculations Week 2:

Week two starts off with the Morrison Project, for projects that are not completed on the day they start like the Lander Project, we use the base pay for the hours worked as a P4P placeholder until it's complete.
Mon = $15.00 BP x 5.8 CT (Morrison Project Placeholder)
Mon = $87.00 P4P PH

Tue = $15.00 BP x 6.4 CT (Morrison Project Placeholder)
Tue = $96.00 P4P PH

Wednesday the Morrison Project is completed, now we can calculate Dale's portion of P4P. He also had a 2 person mow route.

Part 1:
For Morrison Project
Wed = (12.2 (personal clocked time) / 31.1 (Total clocked time) x 32 (Budgeted Hours) x $70 (hourly rate charged) x .33 (% labor revenue)) - ($87.00 Mon PH +$96.00 Tuc PH)

Wed = (12.2 PCT / 31.1 TCT x 32 BH x $70 HRC x .33 LR%) - ($183.00 PH)
Wed = $106.97 P4P

Part 2:
For the 2 person mow route:
Wed = (5.92 BH x $70 HRC x .33 LR%) / 2 P
Wed = $68.38 P4P

Wed = $175.35 Total day P4P

Thursday we started the Burgess Project, it was not completed that day.

Thur = $15.00 BP x 5.1 CT (Burgess Project Placeholder)
Thur = $76.50 P4P PH

Friday the Burgess Project is completed, we can now calculate his P4P portion.

Fri = (10.4 PCT / 34.5 TCT x 32 BH x $70 HRC x .33 LR%) - ($76.50 PH Thur)
Fri = $146.33 P4P

We'll add up the total for Wk 2, Dale made $581.18 P4P.
His total P4P for this Pay Period is $1,090.44.

While the P4P is calculated, we know for Week 1 his total hours was 39.97; multiplied by his base pay equals $599.55. Week 2 his total hours was 33.47; multiplied by base pay is $502.05; bring the sum of weeks 1 & 2 to $1,101.60

<u>We'll come back to Andy, for now let's calculate Joseph's P4P for week 1.</u>

Joseph was training Dale this week, while training we awarded a +$4/hr Training Bonus to the P4P calculation.

Sat/Sun = ($4 x 3.4 Hr TB) + ((3.22 BH x $70 HRC x .33 LR%) / 2 P)
Sat/Sun = $13.60 TB + $37.19
Sat/Sun = $50.79 P4P

      Monday has a lot going on, remember the importance of calculating each portion "separately" before adding the totals together. Let's break down how we would put our equations together. We'll need a total of 3 equations combined to calculate his P4P, the Training Bonus Equation, the 2 person mow route Equation, and the solo mow route equation.

Mon = ($4 x 9.9 Hr TB) + ((9.44 BH x $70 HRC x .33 LR%) / 2 P) + (.75 BH x $70 HRC x .33 LR%)
   | Training Bonus | | 2 Person Mow Route | | Solo Mow Route |
Mon = $39.60 TB + $109.03 + $17.34
Mon = $165.97 P4P

Tue = ($4 x 9.5 Hr TB) + ((9.26 BH x $70 HRC x .33 LR%) / 2 P) + (1.75 BH x $70 HRC x .33 LR%)
Tue = $38.00 TB + $106.95 + $40.42
Tue = $185.38 P4P

Wed = ($4 x 9.8 Hr TB) + ((8.99 BH x $70 HRC x .33 LR%) / 2 P) + (.5 BH x $70 HRC x .33 LR%)
Wed = $39.20 TB + $103.83 + $11.55
Wed = $154.58 P4P

Thursday has another factor, all we need to do is add the new equation to our calculations.

Thur = ($4 x 8.9 Hr TB) + ((3.59 BH x $70 HRC x .33 LR%) / 3 P) + ((3.33 BH x $70 HRC x .33 LR%) / 2 P) + (1 BH x $70 HRC x .33 LR%)
Thur = $35.60 TB + $27.64 + $38.46 + $23.10
Thur = $124.80 P4P

Fri = ($4 x 9.8 Hr TB) + ((7.46 BH x $70 HRC x .33 LR%) / 2 P) + (2.58 BH x $70 HRC x .33 LR%)
Fri = $39.2 TB + $86.16 + $59.60
Fri = $184.96 P4P

The total P4P for Joseph Week 1 is $866.48.

Joseph's P4P Calculations Week 2:

Mon = ($4 x 9.7 Hr TB) + ($15.00 BP x 8.7 CT (Morrison Project PH))
Mon = $38.80 TB + $130.50 PH
Note, we are keeping the Training Bonus and the Placeholder SEPARATE, we do not want to take away his training bonus when calculating the project's P4P later.

Tue = ($4 x 9.7 Hr TB) + ($15.00 BP x 8.7 CT (Morrison Project PH))
Tue = $38.80 TB + $130.50 PH

Wed = ($4 x 9.5 Hr TB) + ((18.9 PCT / 31.1 TCT x 32 BH x $70 HRC x .33 LR%) - ($130.50 PH Mon + $130.50 PH Tue)) + ((5.92 BH x $70 HRC x .33 LR%) / 2 P)
Wed = $38.00 TB + $188.22 + $68.38
Wed = $294.60 P4P

Pause for a moment and make sure this day's calculations make sense; in particular the project calculation portion. If we are to award the Training Bonus, we have to make sure that bonus is not taken out of his P4P when the project is complete. If you calculated Wednesday on your own and got the total 110.62, you forgot to keep the previous day's placeholders separate from the bonus.

Thur = ($4 x 9.1 Hr TB) + ($15.00 BP x 8.1 CT (Burgess Project PH))
Thur = $36.40 TB + $121.50 PH

Fri = ($4 x 8.9 Hr TB) + ((16.1 PCT / 34.5 TCT x 32 BH x $70 HRC x .33 LR%) - ($121.50 PH Thur))
Fri = $35.60 TB + $223.46
Fri = $259.06 P4P

  Joseph's P4P total for Week 2 is $1,050.16, add this with Week 1 and his overall P4P for this Pay Period is $1,916.64.

Calculating is Base Pay, the first weeks hours are 50.92, the second weeks hours were 46.70- If we want to plug these into the Base Pay equation it would look like this:
Total Base Pay = (40 Hr x $15.00 BP + 10.92 Hr x $22.50 OT)wk 1 + (40 Hr x $15.00 BP + 6.7 Hr x $22.50 OT) wk 2
Total Base Pay = $845.70 wk 1 + $750.75 wk 2
Total Base Pay = $1,596.45

  Compile these together, and we have our Payroll Summary.

Payroll Summary

EMP.	P4P Total	Base Pay Rate	Base Pay Total	Total Hours	OT Hours	OT Pay	Bonus*
Joseph	$1,916.64	$15.00	$1,596.45	97.62	17.62	$396.45	$452.34
Andy	?	$15.00	?	?	?	?	?
Dale	$1,090.44	$15.00	$1,101.60	73.44	0	$0.00	$0.00
Thomas	$581.43	$15.00	$482.10	32.14	0	$0.00	$99.33

The "Bonus" is the P4P total, minus the Base Pay Rate, times the Total Hours; if the P4P Total is greater. If the Base Pay Total was higher than P4P, we would pay out the Base Pay Total and there wouldn't be a "bonus".

Concept Check; Andy's P4P Calculations

Test Your Knowledge, and calculate Andy's P4P.

We'll start you off with Monday's Equation, fill in the blanks and calculate his P4P for week 1 and week 2.

Mon = (_____ BH x $70 HRC x .33 LR%)
Mon = $ _____ P4P

Tue =
Tue = $ _____ P4P

Wed =
Wed = $ _____ P4P

Thur =
Thur =
Thur = $ _____ P4P

Fri =
Fri =
Fri = $ _____ P4P

Andy's Total P4P for Week 1 is: $ _____

Andy's P4P Week 2 Calculations; I'll start you off with Monday again:

Mon = ($4 x _____ TB) + ((_____ BH x $70 HRC x .33 LR%) / 2 P) - $125.00 Damage Case
Mon = _____ TB + _____ - $125.00 Damage Case
Mon = $ _____ P4P

Tue =
Tue =
Tue = $ _____ P4P

Wed =
Wed =
Wed = $ _____ P4P

Thur =
Thur = $ _____ P4P

Fri =
Fri = $ _____ P4P

Andy's Total P4P for Week 2 is: $ _____ P4P

Andy's Total P4P for this Pay Period is: $ _____
Andy's Total Hours for week 1 was 42.07, and his total hours for week 2 were 45.57.

Calculate his base pay.

Total Base Pay =
Total Base Pay =
Total Base Pay =

Complete the Payroll Summary.

Payroll Summary

EMP.	P4P Total	Base Pay Rate	Base Pay Total	Total Hours	OT Hours	OT Pay	Bonus*
Joseph	$1,916.64	$15.00	$1,596.45	97.62	17.62	$396.45	$452.34
Andy	$	$15.00	$			$	$
Dale	$1,090.44	$15.00	$1,101.60	73.44	0	$0.00	$0.00
Thomas	$581.43	$15.00	$482.10	32.14	0	$0.00	$99.33

For the full breakdown of Andy's P4P calculations, see Appendix D.

Solutions to Andy's P4P
Appendix D

Sample Week 1

EMP.	Joseph	Andy	Dale	Thomas
Sat/Sun	$50.79 *Training Bonus (+$4/hr, 3.4 Hr) (3.22 BH 2 P Mow)		$37.19 (3.22 BH 2 P Mow)	
Mon	$165.97 *Training Bonus (+$4/hr, 9.9 Hr) (9.44 BH 2 P Mow) (.75 BH Solo Mow)	**$184.80** (8 BH Solo)	$109.03 (9.44 BH 2 P Mow)	
Tue	$185.38 *Training Bonus (+$4/hr, 9.5 Hr) (9.26 BH 2 P Mow) (1.75 BH Solo Mow)	**$184.80** (8 BH Solo)	$106.95 (9.26 BH 2 P Mow)	
Wed	$154.58 *Training Bonus (+$4/hr, 9.8 Hr) (8.99 BH 2 P Mow) (.5 BH Solo Mow)	**$309.31** (13.39 BH Solo)	$103.83 (8.99 BH 2 P Mow)	
Thur	$124.80 *Training Bonus (+$4/hr, 8.9 Hr) (3.59 BH 3 P Mow) (3.33 BH 2 P Mow) (1 BH Solo Mow)	**$99.94** (3.59 BH 3 P Mow) (3.13 BH Solo Mow)	$66.10 (3.59 BH 3 P Mow) (3.33 BH 2 P Mow)	
Fri	$184.96 *Training Bonus (+$4/hr, 9.8 Hr) (7.46 BH 2 P Mow) (2.58 BH Solo Mow)	**$248.10** *Training Bonus (+$4/hr, 8 Hr) *Lander Project (9.36 CT)	$86.16 (7.46 BH 2 P Mow)	$216.10 *Lander Project (9.36 CT)

Sample Week 2

EMP.	Joseph	Andy	Dale	Thomas
Sat/ Sun				
Mon	$169.30 *Training Bonus (+$4/hr, 9.7 Hr) *Morrison Project (8.7 CT)	**$30.78** *Training Bonus (+$4/hr, 8.8 Hr) *Damage Case: -$125.00 (10.44 BH 2 P Mow)	$87.00 *Morrison Project (5.8 CT)	$120.58 (10.44 BH 2 P Mow)
Tue	$169.30 *Training Bonus (+$4/hr, 9.7 Hr) *Morrison Project (8.7 CT)	**$162.11** *Training Bonus (+$4/hr, 9.4 Hr) (10.78 BH 2 P Mow)	$96.00 *Morrison Project (6.4 CT)	$124.51 (10.78 BH 2 P Mow)
Wed	$294.60 *Training Bonus (+$4/hr, 9.5 Hr) *Morrison Project COMPLETE (8.7 CT) (5.92 BH 2 P Mow)	**$154.64** *Training Bonus (+$4/hr, 8.6 Hr) (10.41 BH 2 P Mow)	$175.35 (5.92 BH 2 P Mow) (Morrison Project Complete)	$120.24 (10.41 BH 2 P Mow)
Thur	$157.90 *Training Bonus (+$4/hr, 9.1 Hr) *Burgess Project (8.1 CT)	**$216.45** (9.37 BH Solo Mow)	$76.50 *Burgess Project (5.1 CT)	
Fri	$259.06 *Training Bonus (+$4/hr, 8.9 Hr) *Burgess Project COMPLETE (8 CT)	**$171.41** *Burgess Project COMPLETE (8 CT)	$146.33 *Burgess Project COMPLETE (5.3 CT)	

Mon = (8 BH x $70 HRC x .33 LR%)
Mon = $ 184.80 P4P

Tue = (8 BH x $70 HRC x .33 LR%)
Tue = $ 184.80 P4P

Wed = (13.39 BH x $70 HRC x .33 LR%)
Wed = $ 309.31 P4P

Thur = ((3.59 BH x $70 HRC x .33 LR%) / 3 P) + (3.13 BH x $70 HRC x .33 LR%)
Thur = $27.64 + $72.30
Thur = $ 99.94 P4P

Fri = ($4 x 8 Hr TB) + (9.355 PCT / 18.71 TCT x 18.71 BH x $70 HRC x .33 LR%) - $0.00 PH
 Fri = $32.00 TB + $216.10
Fri = $ 248.10 P4P

Andy's Total P4P for Week 1 is: $ 1,026.95 .

Andy's P4P Week 2 Calculation Solutions:

Mon = ($4 x 8.8 Hr TB) + ((10.44 BH x $70 HRC x .33 LR%) / 2 P) - $125.00 Damage Case
Mon = $35.2 TB + $120.58 - $125.00 Damage Case
Mon = $ 30.78 P4P

Tue = ($4 x 9.4 Hr TB) + ((10.78 BH x $70 HRC x .33 LR%) / 2 P)
Tue = $37.60 TB + $124.51
Tue = $ 162.11 P4P

Wed = ($4 x 8.6 Hr TB) + ((10.41 BH x $70 HRC x .33 LR%) / 2 P)
Wed = $34.40 TB + $120.24
Wed = $ 154.64 P4P

Thur = (9.37 BH x $70 HRC x .33 LR%)
Thur = $ 216.45 P4P

Fri = (8 PCT / 34.5 TCT x 32 BH x $70 HRC x .33 LR%) – ($0.00 PH)
Fri = $ 171.41 P4P

Andy's Total P4P for Week 2 is: $ 735.39 .

Andy's Total P4P for this Pay Period is: $ 1,762.34 .

Total Base Pay = (40 Hr x $15.00 BP + 2.07 Hr x $22.50 OT) wk 1 + (40 Hr x $15.00 BP + 5.57 Hr x $22.50 OT) wk 2
Total Base Pay = $646.58 wk 1 + $725.33 wk 2
Total Base Pay = $1,371.91 BP

Finally, we can compile all of this information to create a pay stub for this pay period:

Payroll Summary

EMP.	P4P Total	Base Pay Rate	Base Pay Total	Total Hours	OT Hours	OT Pay	Bonus*
Joseph	$1,916.64	$15.00	$1,596.45	97.62	17.62	$396.45	$452.34
Andy	$1,762.34	$15.00	$1,371.91	87.64	7.64	$171.90	$447.74
Dale	$1,090.44	$15.00	$1,101.60	73.44	0	$0.00	$0.00
Thomas	$581.43	$15.00	$482.10	32.14	0	$0.00	$99.33

Ps. Once you sign up for your free trial (with the code previously given in the book) at P4Psoftware.com you can book a video call with one of our team. They will help you with P4P implementation and figuring out the numbers for your specific business, concerning base pay and percent of revenue share with the employees.

Compiled Figures & Diagrams

Fig.1

Hourly Rate to the Customer	Base Pay Maximum Recommendation
$60/hr	$15/hr
$65/hr	$16.25/hr
$70/hr	$17.5/hr
$75/hr	$18.75/hr
$80/hr	$20/hr
$85/hr	$21.25/hr

Fig.2

Date: 10/31/21

Territory: Coquitlam BC

Client Name, City & State: **Phillips, Zach**   123 Augusta Pl

Compaint or Issue: Missed edging in the back yard by the dog run.

Resolution: Return to complete edging.

Owned By: Mike Andes

Serviced By: Liz Naber

Fig.3

---

12 MONTH CONTRACT:

1.) Mowing:
   a. Weekly Visits March-June / Sept.-Nov.
   b. Bi-Weekly Visits July-August
   c. Includes Knocking Down Grass on Hillside Along First Street
   d. Includes All Other Lawn Areas
(($140 (weekly price) x 26 (visits)
+ 210 (biweekly price) x 8 (visits) = $5,320))

2.) Weeding:
   a. Bi-Weekly Visits March-Nov.
   b. Pull Large Weeds in Garden Beds
   c. Remove Garbage and Debris
   d. Spray Areas of Heavy Weed Growth
   e. Blow Off Parking Lots
(($300 spray + $90 (biweekly price) x 20 (visits) = $2,100))

3.) Tree and Bush Trimming:
   a. To be Completed in March, August and November
   b. Trim and Shape Bushes lining Walkways and Driveway
   c. Trim Any Low Hanging Branches from Magnolias
   d. Trim Bushes or Trees That Are Touching the Siding of Homes to Reduce Algae/Rodents
   e. Haul Away Work Related Debris
   f. Video Recorded for Service Crew
(($420 (Per Visit) x 3 (visits) = $1,260))

(($8,680 TOTAL / 12 Months = $723.33))

Fig. 4

Example Time Card: Week 1 of Pay Period

Day	BH for Route	Actual Time to Complete	Calculated P4P (Daily)	Base Pay (Daily)
Mon	8.5	9	182.33	135.00
Tue	8.5	9.25	182.33	138.75
Wed	9	9	193.05	135.00
Thur	8	9	171.60	135.00
Fri	8.5	9.5	182.33	56.25 + 129.38 OT
TOTALS	**42.5**	**45.75**	**911.64**	**729.38**

Fig. 5

Example Time Card: Week 2 of Pay Period

Day	BH for Route	Actual Time to Complete	Calculated P4P (Daily)	Base Pay (Daily)
Mon	8.5	6.8	182.33	102.00
Tue	8.5	7.5	182.33	112.50
Wed	9	7.9	193.05	118.50
Thur	8	7.5	171.60	112.50
Fri	8.5	8	182.33	120.00
TOTALS	**42.5**	**37.7**	**911.64**	**565.50**

Fig. 6

P4P Grand Totals:	Base Pay Grand Totals:
• Week 1 total: 911.64 • Week 2 total: 911.64	• Week 1 total: 600.00 • 129.38 Overtime • Week 2 total: 565.50
$1,823.28 P4P	**$1,294.88 Base Pay**

Fig. 7

Employee: Zach Phillips	Date: Example week 1 - week 2
Hours: 77.7 Base Pay (15.00/hr): 1,165.50 P4P Bonus: 528.40	Overtime Hours: 5.75 Overtime: 129.38 Manual Adjustments: 0.00 **Total Pay: 1,823.28**

Fig. 8

Example Time Card: Week 1 of 2nd Pay Period

Day	BH for Route	Actual Time to Complete	Calculated P4P (Daily)	Base Pay (Daily)
Mon	7.33*	7	105.00 ->	105.00
Tue	7.33*	8	120.00 ->	120.00
Wed	7.33*	5.5	246.90** Mezinger Project Complete	82.50
Thur	8	7.5	171.60	112.50
Fri	8.5	8	182.33	120.00
TOTALS	**38.49**	**36**	**$825.83**	**$540.00**

Fig. 9

Daily Report Card	**Name:** Jack Keen **Date:** 10-09-21
Hours Clocked In: 10.00	**Project Name:** Johnson House
Base Pay Earned: $120.00	**Project Budgeted Hours:** 15
P4P Earned: $231.00	**Total Project Worked Hours:** 1
Manual Adjustments: $0.00	**Project Status:** Started
Notes:	

Fig. 10

Name	Score	$Per/Hr Earned	Total Budgeted Hours	Total Revenue
Jason	4.52	$29.98	43.75	$3365.00
Tim	4.61	$26.02	36.88	$2894.42
John	4.64	$24.15	23.42	$1849.81

Fig. 11

	Losing Money	Break Even	Profitable
Score	1-2	2	Above 3

Fig. 12

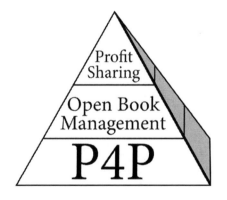

Made in the USA
Columbia, SC
29 April 2024

521b628e-c612-4372-9dc8-375a450552d5R01